backscatter

ALSO BY JOHN OLSON

The Night I Dropped Shakespeare on the Cat, 2006
Free Stream Velocity, 2004
Echo Regime, 2000
Eggs & Mirrors, 1999
Logo Lagoon, 1999
Swarm of Edges, 1996

backscatter

New and Selected Poems

John Olson

Black Widow Press
Boston, MA

BLACK WIDOW PRESS is an imprint of Commonwealth Books, Inc., Boston. All Black Widow Press books are printed on acid-free paper, glued and sewn into bindings.

JOSEPH S. PHILLIPS, Publisher
www.blackwidowpress.com

Cover Design by Derek White
Book Design by Kerrie Kemperman
Title font, Grit Primer, by Eduardo Recife

ISBN-13: 978-09795137-3-2
ISBN-10: 09795137-3-1

Library of Congress Cataloging-in-Publication Data

Olson, John, 1947–
    Backscatter / John Olson. — Black Widow Press ed.
    p. cm.
    ISBN-13: 978-09795137-3-2
    I. Title

Printed by Thomson-Shore
Printed in the United States

10 9 8 7 6 5 4 3 2 1

for Roberta

TABLE OF CONTENTS

This Other World: An Essay On Artistic Autonomy ● 11

The Bell of Madness ● 19

City of Words ● 22

Some Things I Have Said ● 25

Some Wanton Reflections ● 27

The Night I Dropped Shakespeare On The Cat ● 29

The Mystery of Grocery Carts ● 33

Our Feelings Reach Out Beyond Us ● 35

Philip Lives: A Lament For Lamantia ● 41

Missoula ● 44

Gertrude Stein Again And Again ● 48

A Trip To The Library ● 50

Aesopian Smelt ● 52

A Big Noise ● 53

Meniscus ● 55

Point-Blank And Scraggily ● 57

Casus Belli ● 58

Inclined ● 60

Sit Anywhere ● 62

An Accidental Treatise On The Paragraph Glands of Gravy Canyon ● 64

Dubuffet Buffet ● 66

Sale ● 68

Current ● 70

There Was A Time ● 78

Better Homes And Abstractions ● 80

Squirt ● 81

Yogurt ● 82

New Grind ● 84

Transient Notion ● 85

A Brain ● 87

Marsden Hartley's Gloves ● 89

Color Noctambule ● 91

Crocus ● 92

Miro's Blues ● 96

Eve's Medium ● 104

Moulin Bleu ● 105

Trembling Gobbets of Language ● 107

Mercury ● 109

Restrictions Unbound ● 111

Contrabassoon ● 115

Bagpipe ● 117

Red Guitars ● 119

Xylophone ● 121

Prose Sonata in G-Flat ● 123

Morning Arrival ● 129

I Was An Extra On *Gunsmoke* ● 131

Captain Nemo Serves Professor Aronnax ● 133

Alphabet Soup ● 135

My Favorite Gland ● 139

Curiosity Was Born With The Universe ● 141

City Of Water ● 142

Gray's Anatomy ● 143

Hundreds Of Old Men Marching In The Rain In Belgium ● 145

Bienvenue ● 146

Free Will Is Not A Profession ● 148

Cell Abrasion ● 150

Swimming Is Not Enough ● 152

Kinema ● 155

Arthur Rimbaud On Horseback ● 159

Apropos of Fruit ● 161

Eight Or Nine Reasons To Carry A Loaded Jaw ● 162

Mansion Of Mint ● 164

The Prodigality of Green ● 166

What We Are What Are We ● 168

The Taste Of Ocher Forth ● 171

Grave 53 ● 195

THIS OTHER WORLD:
AN ESSAY ON ARTISTIC AUTONOMY

The exhilaration of poetry is in its gall, its brassy irrelevance and gunpowder vowels, its pulleys and popcorn and delirious birds. It is transcendent yet wild, a whirl of energy in a shell of sound. A leopard of thought moving with stealth through a jungle of words.

The poem is not a tool. It is a rehearsal for dying. Mortality is a cage. Unless one crawls out of one's skin to find the air quick and immediate and ready to do one's bidding one cannot attain the conjurer's art. Ariel remains trapped in a tree. Caliban becomes CEO of Merck.

The poet sits down to write: luscious roots climb down through the earth nuclear and moist moving toward definition, the brightness of an apple. The poet goes into a trance. The poet becomes entrenched in absorption. Disembodiment. Abstractions boil out of the pen, a laughing eruptive heat animates a cart for selling hot dogs. Daylight spilling through a window. A sunflower bursting out of the ground. A Saturday buttered with intellect. A Thursday buttressed with edelweiss.

In its ardent claim for autonomy the poem becomes an embarrassment, a swashbuckling rascal flamboyant as Errol Flynn. What does it mean? Does it mean anything? Is there wisdom in it? Is there an epiphany fenced in its meadow like a unicorn? Or does it snidely snicker at the whole idea of a theme, a redemptive prune of healthful understanding? The poem quietly undoes a bolt and slips through the door. It escapes. It migrates south, and settles on a pond in Pennsylvania to preen its commas and metaphors.

Art's autonomy remains irrevocable. All efforts to restore art by giving it a social function—of which art is itself uncertain and by which it expresses its own uncertainty—are doomed (Adorno 1).

Find a poem. Hold it in your hand. Is it warm? Is it cold? Does it throb? Does it squirm? That molten rock rising to the surface looks dangerous. Better step back.

If prose is a living room, the poem is a closet, a marginalized space where ghostly inflections hang like clothes. A lapel of morning, a sleeve of death.

The poem is best kept out of sight. It is terrible in its autonomy. It has the capacity to create an infinite number of meanings. A refrain shattered by striving to say something new litters the floor. The metabolism of a backyard woodpile smolders with composting heat. Decay and creation combine to produce an imbroglio of paradox and wax. Bees moving in and out of a hive. Words moving in and out of a mind. How far do they go? Do they go beyond this world? Yes, yes, they do. They go beyond this world. They go where they go. They go orange. They go rampant. They go elsewhere.

Only by virtue of separation from empirical reality, which sanctions art to model the relation of the whole and the part according to the work's own need, does the artwork achieve a heightened order of existence (Adorno 4).

Words are bees. They buzz. They sting. They collect pollen. They make wax and honey. They navigate by distance (visual input from the ground), and the amount of energy they have expended. They are not entirely autonomous. They require a horizon, a hive, a design. They may create anything. Pinch the air. Squeeze meaning and galaxies of sound out of it. Pin the flavor of oblivion to the palates of our mouths. Click and clatter and roll and bounce. Bulge with oranges. Assumes shapes, cruets, crowbars, rhythms and bells that dance in the night. Swim, swarm, spin. Bring us to the frontier of perception. Mirror the fugues of the soul. But hold to their design. Their polymers. Their interactions.

Art is autonomous and it is not; without what is heterogeneous to it, its autonomy eludes it (Adorno 6).

Imagine a volcano, a semantic wildness turning red. What does it tell you? The eruptive force of the poem is why it is both revered and ignored, exalted and set aside within an industrial society. Industry requires obedience. The poem exalts disobedience. Dissonance. Dissent. Sincerity.

Art is the social antithesis of society, not directly deducible from it (Adorno 8).

The poem must never be politic. Not if it is to be impulsive, wiggly, and maniacal. A calamity coincident as gooseberries, consonants smacked into vowels. Meat dripping with emotion. An inflammation alive as an olive and ugly as a Wednesday afternoon. The roar of rapids scraps of food tossed to the crows and sparrows. Strings deliriously stroked on the neck of a guitar.

By virtue of its rejection of the empirical world—a rejection that inheres in art's concept and thus is no mere escape, but a law immanent to it—art sanctions the primacy of reality (Adorno 2).

Lyricism is lame. Lyricism is virtuosity. Lyricism is to poetry what malaria is to the jungle explorer.

The poem, busy within its fiber, licks the walls of the city with the specular color of giants and fairies, beauty sprayed from a bottle, totems on a remote Alaskan shore, incantations that awaken powerful healing energies. The chemistry is strange, but derivative. It grows like lettuce on an asteroid. It proposes a new constellation of sense. The clarity of a snowshoe on the wall. A hot shower after a cold day in the snow. A tin whistle letting out the latitude of a foreign clime. The sparkling energies of rhapsodic lobsters singing a cappella disasters of African mahogany.

In each genuine artwork something appears that does not exist (Adorno 82).

Gathering cellophane once is sword. Gathering cellophane twice is pudding. It is either existential to stand in the sand, or abusively silk, like an acciaccatura held open by hoops. Life is a confrontation with its own cubicle. It's a twist of incision to insinuate rose when a blown bark means dimple. There are never enough kinds of intestine when a trumpet crashes through the abdomen evolving hints of music as a species of food or love or tomahawk. There are too many words in the previous sentence. It reads like a race for horses entered as competitors before their birth to the King of Athens. The quality of being futile is an asset to the governance of suds. As a yellow clock parts timidly with its time, the air stream on the outskirts of town gather all the crickets together in a nebulae of rubbed wings. Or whatever it is that makes that sound. Sometimes the world gets caught in your writing and you don't know what to do with it while on other occasions you can't absolve the dawn with enough infatuation, or Flemish grisaille. Like it or not we are stuck with the empirical world. But you can always go camping, catch some trout, slice it up, put it in a pan with a little butter and voila! existence slips through its shackles of chervil and chintz to glimpse something bright and original at the end of a fork. The glitter of light on a lake. The milky reverie of a clarinet. The grammar of prestidigitation. The vibrato of a larch.

Reach down, reach down deep and bring a width of something drastic and wild out of your throat. Laughter, crying, anguish, speech. Dogma beaten into skulls. Icicles, cactus, syllables. A brain of steam. The call of a moose. Blood on a blade. Northern lights a ghostly moan. People at a table eating lasagna. Cosmic nebulae a Gothic cathedral on the French plains. A clock sagging with the lassitude of time.

The resistance to empirical reality that the subject marshals in the autonomous work is at the same time resistance to the immediate appearance of nature (Adorno 66).

It takes a hand to glisten on the stones. It takes a magnet of distant neon to create a cowlick, a glissando of apricots palpable as paradise yet ethereal as a junkyard. Varnish the canvas and paint a flag. A woman wearing an apron on Sunday. An indigo dye accommodating the construction of a blister. Daylight trickling through the sonnet refinery.

Stones blasted from a wall of rock.

A metabolism slipping through its bundle of life evokes that bolt. You can slide it back if you want. There is a hemisphere on the other side. The wall will ever bump itself until the light of heaven percolates through the flab of our daily realm. Merchandise those blossoms you believe will turn the scale upside down. There is no way to quantify poetry. If you're looking for something to do rummage around in the G-strings. Bag another propeller and fly a buffalo to Utica.

With human means art wants to realize the language of what is not human (Adorno 78).

What is not human is most certainly mittens. When daylight is massed on the horizon at dawn that's our cue to begin sprinkling our legs with mushrooms and flowers. Fill the lighthouse with the echoing sounds of our madcap vowels. The geometry of dirt is neither gauze nor acorn but a bikini worn by provocation at the far end of a dirt road in Texas.

There is an energy in everyone that is clear and sweet and wild until it is twisted into dimes.

Dharma is a portable wilderness.

Each time we read a text we deepen its meaning. Words newly constellated bring about a singularity of meaning. To create a work of art is to remake an intellectual order of the world.

The poem creates a space for the gravitational force of its words. Their semantic weight comes from the dirt in which they grow, the chains against which they tug and strain. Diadem, harmony, hand. Words newly constellated plucked like strings
on a harp.

The more that art is thoroughly organized as an object by the subject and divested of the subject's intentions, the more articulately does it speak according to the model of a nonconceptual, non rigidified signification of language (Adorno 67).

The more perfect the artwork, the more it forsakes intentions (Adorno 78).

Only till meaning seeps through the words does something akin to architecture begin to stir with exposition. Gigantic lianas hang down from the tops of enormous trees. Difficulties gamut into grooves of jeep and chassis. The expedition halts momentarily to take its measure.

Is it time to build? What shall we construct?

Vowels are the trowels by which we layer the mortar of sound. We think they are stable habitations. But they are not. They are emperor moths, sow bugs, incandescent polymorphic reliquaries of remembrance and reverie. No, they are not stable. They are not even easily oxidized. Because they are made of words, which are operations of impulse, demands for immediate satisfaction. Jam. Jelly. Components of moistened crumpet.

We cannot control the monsters we create. But that's precisely the joy of it all. The wildness of the energy released.

Artworks detach themselves from the empirical world and bring forth another world, one opposed to the empirical world as if this other world too were an autonomous entity (Adorno 1).

Go, go forth harpsichord ghost and play a lambent rhapsody of rings and spoons and late night diners of cherry pie dishevelment. An age attired in dials blisters the omission of scope. The oyster is an engine of calm. Hang that meaning inside yourself and seethe with personality. Being is all lunge and fire, a lean star of acetylene. Make that need to intensify experience go whistle its song to the highway. Madam macadam is calling you. She says distance is an illusion. It is speed that matters. The velocity of language. The temperature of brass. Saw what is existential in half and make a dragon out of it. Add nails. Add pounding. Add a naked memory snapped like incense in a fit of acoustic purple. Say what you need. Dress your lips in a husky licorice of happy abandon. The arrival will amaze you. The glass will reflect you. The words will release you.

Work Cited

Adorno, Theodore. *Aesthetic Theory.* University of Minnesota Press, 1977.

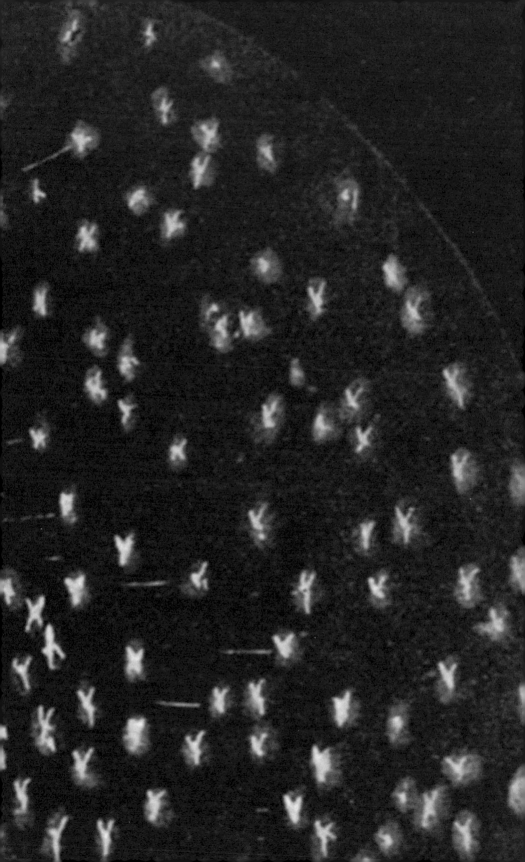

THE BELL OF MADNESS

Back in the sixties I was in my twenties.

I was nineteen in '66 when The Rolling Stones came out with a slew of hits, "Paint It Black" and "Under My Thumb" and "Time Is On My Side." This was the year Norv and I drove out west in a black '55 Chevy dreaming of girls and drugs and sunny California.

I was 48,000 light years away from where I was born.

I was in San Francisco, city of garlic and spiders and Mozart's nose. City of splendor. City of fog and mental landscapes baked in poetry. City of the Six Gallery and City Lights and *Howl*. City of the golden bridge and fisherman's wharf and trophoblastic druids riding glass dragons and stroking the velvet penis of a locomotive valentine.

And Coit Tower and the city aquarium and Madam Tussaud's wax breasts weren't enough for me.

Because I was such a hot and crazy teenager. And in America everyone gets to be a teenager until they turn 40. This is a full quarter century of teenaging. A full quarter century of shenanigans and volcanic ejaculations and blazing hardware and fruit. And although the government strongly encouraged me to go to a distant country and shoot people I said no I don't want to go to a distant country and shoot people why would I want to go to a distant country and shoot people when they're not coming over here and shooting at me or even threatening to come over here and shoot at me or shoot at you or shoot at anyone else walking the streets of Monterey or Petaluma or Manhattan I want to sit on the dock of the bay I want to be a teenager I want to hone my consonants and vowels into guns of breath into guns that shoot wild brilliant metaphors and cause heavenly disruption and bluebells and leopards. Most of all I want to be a beatnik!

Like Jack Kerouac!

Like Philip Lamantia!

Like Michael McClure!

This was my greatest ambition. To write a great poem like one of the great poems in Donald Allen's anthology *The New American*

Poetry. Which I completely fell in love with. Which sustained me spiritually and psychologically for decades.

My heart burned like a mushrooming borscht of Rabelaisian vitality. I had to construct a poem as terrific and complex as a chromosome. Or a cockatoo. Or the chromosome of a cockatoo.

A cockatoo at sunset.

A cockatoo at dawn.

A cockatoo preening its feathers at noon.

The nights were huge then and the days were long and buoyant. My eyes clutched the shirt of the sky. I was writing such terrible poetry it clanked like a bad muffler. I didn't know how to gun the engine. I was still learning to shift gears.

San Francisco was like a huge wedding cake iced with fog and purple haze, St. Francis of Assisi cathedral and the wonderful extravagance of the streets, whose irregularity corresponded to the clouds. And clang clang went the trollies.

An old monk read passages from Rimbaud. I was hungry. And I was learning how to interpret symbols and omens. I saw crows everywhere, and starlings drunk on fermented berries. I waddled around like Baudelaire's albatross.

All my memories of that time are made for the night. They come out at night and make me feel young and promiscuous again. Like crickets and stars. And sticks on a drum. Sticks pounding beats on a drum. Sticks pounding tender buttons on a drum.

Still, I was a really bad poet. I didn't know how to shoulder a harbor or squeeze liquid into a tube of hot Mexican sound. I didn't know what an Appaloosa was. I thought it was some kind of horse. I didn't know it was a cathedral of bone. And when I discovered it was a cathedral of bone I didn't know it was actually a horse.

And all those days and all those people and all those aspirations were a beverage. I wanted to drink them all and then spit them out as poetry. All those windows and all those streets. All those license plates and all those fish. All that breath and meat and armor. All those clouds crawling over the hills to turn into nasturtiums at the bottom of the valley. At the bottom of Lombard. I would have liked to have ripped them out and made electricity out of them. Youth requires grandeur.

One day I saw Egypt walk by clutching a ghost.

And the sun was a peach bleeding light and heat and cumulus and wheat.

And the moon was a color whose corollary was gauze and whose chasteness was cold as the plumbing of heaven.

And the common was strange and the strange was common.

The whole country went mad. The televisions spewed images of bombs and bonfires and bonitos and brains. I saw images of Vietnam the wounded carried on stretchers. Young men began to return home missing legs and arms and sanity.

It sounded like a lot of people were dying over there.

And the bell of madness that jingles like a final desire in the bluish air.

That's a line from "The Prose of the Trans-Siberian and of Little Jeanne of France" by Blaise Cendrar. Who also said "we are a storm in the skull of a deaf man." That's a pretty good line, don't you think? Thank you, Blaise, for the great poem. Thank you for the train. Thank you for the clanks and clickety-clank of the wheels and the lurches and phantoms and crows. Thank you for the bell of madness that jingles like a final desire in the bluish air, and thank you for the temperature of your desolation, snickering among the iron in the junkyard of the moon.

CITY OF WORDS

I am a citizen of a city of words. Everything in the city is made of words. Apricots and granaries, fables and wires. Abbeys in the mist. Corner drugstores harboring all the secrets of the body. Longing, injury, pain. Hotels, casinos, department stores. Everything is made of words. Everything is rendered by language. Vowels and consonants surging from the chest. Barges, ferries, and gunboats. A vast horizon wild with swinging cranes, islands of meaning revealing the strange beauty of faucets at night. You name it. If you can feel it, smell it, taste it, climb it, walk on it, or wear it, it is made of words. This is the city of words. What we call light is really words. The mouth of a river assembled from bones and teeth. The air humming with the sound of ghosts.

Many of the words have become frayed from long usage. The city of words is an old city. It has been here ever since the first humans made sounds in reference to other things: fire, water, breath. Birth, death, beauty. You name it. This is the marvel of words. Their meat and bark is virtual. They are best understood as waves moving through the air carrying herring and mushrooms, grievance and gratitude. Smoke from samovars. Bandanas and catalogues. Culture, economy, tourism, sports.

When human beings began to wear clothes, plant grain in fields and build habitations to shelter their exposed and furless bodies from the cold and rain, the city of words attained dizzying heights of grandeur and dream. Camels filled the streets. Wagons lurched forward pulled by mules. Sentences lurched forward propelled by verbs. It wasn't long after that cars were invented. And government and taxes. Human biology moving about everywhere making sounds and raising questions of existence and decency.

Everywhere in the city there are towers of steel and glass. Dials, gauges, valves, pumps, pulleys, pipes. Art galleries drug the afternoon. Buildings and waterways are lit with candles and oil lamps. But this is not the real city. These are only the surface features of the city. The real city is in your mouth. The real city is in a state of being spoken, about to be spoken, or rivers of reverie meandering in candle wax.

There is a library at the heart of the city where many words are stored in books in case of drought or plague. The words are pumped into books by poets and journalists and then placed on shelves in an order arranged by letter and number.

Every morning when the sun rises over the mountains the city of words begins its activities. Tattoo parlors offer rhubarb and conversation. The words in the zoo howl and roar and assume meanings too wild for the restrictions of grammar. Radios exude the glow of music. Stadiums fill with expectancy and hope. Light spreads in all directions. Even the subway turnstiles seem freshly awakened from a night of hollow routine.

During the summer a carnival visits the city. Here one finds cages of savage, untamed words. Words captured at the frontier between dream and experience, perception and reality. Monstrous words. Words with tusks and horns. Words with long necks and sapphire eyes. Words of fire. Words hard as flint and words so perverse and volatile they cannot be pronounced without first being fixed to the ground by chain.

Elsewhere the city is in a mode of continual reconstruction and manufacture. The words of politicians and lawyers, which tend to be supple and light, are used to make bathrobes, curtains, Frisbees, and rubber bands. The grave, heavy words of doctors are used to make fire hydrants, aquariums, waffle irons, and golf carts.

The words of poets cannot be used for anything. They are too hot to handle. Too fugitive and erratic. They are like the subatomic particles which hold reality together, although they themselves have no reality. They are mathematical probabilities, equations, abstract figures. They point to a larger reality than the one we encounter in the physical realm.

➤

Once every few years there is a large conference given in which to discuss two important questions: did humanity create language, or did language create humanity? The first question is pertinent to the second: are we the masters of language, or are we the subjects of language, here to do its bidding?

The fact that we, as citizens of a city of words, argue these points with the very words we are putting into question, does not hinder our discussion. We cannot step out of them long enough to feel what thinking might be like without words. For that, we look to the animals, cats, dogs, dolphins and elephants. We look into their eyes hoping to glimpse something of an alternate world, a consciousness we have lost over time in the process of building our world out of words.

Occasionally, if a word slides into reality and becomes an actual object, such as a whisk broom or daffodil, it is submitted to intense scrutiny and research. It is carried from mouth to mouth and ear to ear as gingerly as an emotion gently maneuvered through a sonnet in order to see if there is a change in its structure or meaning. If words permeate our reality, how might we change our reality to better suit our temperaments?

Here in the city of words there are candy machines in all the gas stations. All the schools are exquisitely public. Nothing is static. Nothing is still. The city of words is not on any map. To get there you simply say something. Time is broken into traffic lights. Gravity gets drunk on motels. We live, we smile, we die. We process sight and smell into sentences. We weave sentences together to make rockets and silk, gyroscopes and crutches. We make pictures with sound. We build telescopes to look at the sky. Stars scintillate in their lenses unveiling a universe of such overwhelming magnitude that language alone cannot do justice to its immeasurable mass and volume. But if one were to view the city of words from elsewhere in space, one would see a scintillation of equal magnitude. A tissue of jewels with no beginning or end.

SOME THINGS I HAVE SAID

There are some things I have said of which I am not altogether confi-
dent. When I said the stones were miniature volcanoes with Kentucky
zippers, I meant Tennessee zephyrs. And when I said the sheer joy of
despair is worth a room at the Waldorf in New York, I meant the
bracelets I am wearing were jails in themselves and that my name
rumbled with trees whenever I resolved to submerge our kitchen in a
perception of liquid. I did mean, with all sincerity and confidence,
that there is a mouth chiseled out of the vapor of the space surround-
ing the beverage of a religious spine of fluorocarbons and ghosts, but
that the image was overcomplicated, and came apart easily, crumbling
apart in the hands like oysters, which are sparkling incidents of fiction
distinct as the wrinkles in your hand. It is true that the dogs of
Minneapolis have been puffed into glass, so that when they bark, or
scratch themselves, or chase a stick of some sort, oak or maple, or
perhaps the broken end of a broom, that the hues within their anato-
my tokened heat and candy. I couldn't help but blurt out the truth of
flowers. Flowers insert descriptions of themselves into the mouth in
such a fashion one cannot help but issue them forth, ventilate them,
trickle lightning from the corners of one's mouth as one's very tongue
moves up and down, and from side to side, inventing names for their
colors and shapes. Blessed is he who carries within himself a gardenia,
an ideal of beauty, and obeys it. I really meant that. But when I said
my elbows were caverns of ice I meant only that they resemble bowls
of disintegrating light, and that when I moved my arms, dollops of
Australia fell through my fingers igniting passionate reds and aborigi-
nal greens, songlines of such tangy extension they feel archived in a
future tense, morning dew stitched into the bikinis of the clouds.
When you return to the kitchen you should shut your eyes, and try to
imagine the sincerity of almonds, the cleverness of salt and the glacial
indifference of sugar. Try to construct an empire of statement, of
things unsaid and yet aching to be uttered, so that when your mouth
opens and the words come out, you will mean them as a swimmer
means to swim, as forms curving and carving their way through the

waves. For nobody doubts the sincerity of waves. They swell into transparency like a grammatical process, the painting of a rice cake that comes and goes, drifting from garage sale to garage sale, creating and leaving impressions, waves and reveries in the mind, various associations having to do with rice, and cake, and painting and representation. This is what I mean to say. This is what I meant to say all along. That there is nothing so pure as a crosswalk in Death Valley, but only cracked mud, blue sky, a regime of sounds and smells that swell into proximity and buoy us up, then pass into the treble of a musician calling out to Ishtar, a pure flame of divinity burning the meat of the sun into a primal mascara, or ratification of green.

SOME WANTON REFLECTIONS

Poetry is the language of crisis. The drugstore pharmacist bleeding on the floor. A soft blue light glimmering up and down his spine.

Johannes Vermeer in a bloodmobile, his sleeve rolled up, various qualities of light playing off the sleeves and collars of the nurses.

Mosques and planetariums.

The songs of Mnemosyne popping open like clams.

Fables of meat and meaning bulging with gerunds. A hungry geometry ravenous for grapes.

The list goes on. Emotions percolate through my body. I have lost track of them. I don't know their names anymore. Rage, elation, acceptance, need. Grackle, chisel, hardtack, kelp.

Bottles get poured and emptied and become impersonal. Some of them are plastic. A few of them are glass. Some of them are dreamlike and have eyebrows crammed with sand.

I reckon a table might be a good place to lactate an eel. But first I must cram my head with words until I know something about borscht and sugar and my forehead bulges with thought and my ribcage epitomizes Michigan.

Is this what I look like? Michigan?

Our mirror has a tendency to invent its own reflections. Yesterday I looked like a peony bloom.

Who are you after all, I say to myself. And why haven't you shaved?

Because every day is a reprieve. And a fugue got caught in my ski boot.

How might we move nearer to the divine? That is the real question.

Right now I can hear the burble and murmur of the dishwasher.

Is that what thought looks like? Steam?

Fingers get inside nouns and turn everything rhetorical. This solves nothing. It is better to keep your fingers out of things and let the words do what they want to do. Today the words would like to reveal something about rain. Is it alive? Is it nervous? Is it public? Is it poetry? →

Yes, yes, yes, and yes. All of the above. It is also a metaphor for death. Water falls from the sky, splatters on the ground, becomes a puddle or a human being, then evaporates and goes back up into the sky.

But where did this sound come from? It is the issue of a yak. Yakkety yak.

I love the word brick. But never punch a wall. Not unless it is a wall of water. And stay away from mirrors. Mirrors are supernatural. They reflect anything. Even rain.

The Night I Dropped Shakespeare
On The Cat

The night I dropped Shakespeare on the cat B.B. King played his
guitar at the south end of Lake Union. He was celebrating his 80th
birthday. Strains of music came through our window. It was a warm
summer evening in mid-August. The moon was out. The stars were
out. I imagined B.B. King's old fingers skillfully tickling the neck of
his guitar a trance a rapture on his face belying all those years. Years
performing and riding a bus. To culminate there above the water his
guitar whining wrestling strains of eternity out of the summer air.
People sitting in the stands. I thought those faint strains of music to
be a stereo left on upstairs. I heard our neighbors go out. I thought
they had left their music on. Their radio maybe. Music playing softly
to an empty room. The presence of music with no one to hear it.
Strains drifting nowhere. But it was B.B. King. B.B. being king. King
of the waters. King of the neck of a guitar. King of the blues. A realm
of sound scrambled and cooked to resemble a sound of mirrors.
Sound is a sound is a sound. We see laminations of time in a sound.
The sound of water. The sound of a guitar. Old fingers rampant and
busy on the neck of a guitar.

    The night I dropped Shakespeare on the cat Mick Jagger appeared
at the end of a news broadcast on TV5 the French television station
we subscribe to so that we can hear French Gallic culture bounced off
a satellite and piped into our apartment Mick Jagger singing with the
Rolling Stones with the usual energy the strutting and thrusting and
jabbing the look of delirium and agitation even in his 60s he looks
young despite the wrinkles the crags of age giving him a peculiarly
rugged look after the androgyny of the 60s he is now *un vieillard
encore vert* an old rugged dinosaur from the 60s still full of fight and
puckish mischief. The man is timeless. His Cheshire grin bright and
sassy as ever. The news had to do with the release of a Stones album
in which Jagger sings with trenchant mockery about the hypocrisy of
the Bush thugs you "you call yourself a Christian/ I think you're a

➔

hypocrite/ you call yourself a patriot/ I think you're a crock of shit."
Crock of shit translated at the bottom of the screen into French *sac du
merde*. Mick explaining the song "Sweet Neo Con" in fluent French
*c'est très clair, tout le monde peut comprendre, mais, voila… c'est pas
personnel.*

The night I dropped Shakespeare on the cat Bush Rice and
Rumsfeld stood at the edge of a dirt road with the Texas prairie in the
background Bush's 1,600 acre ranch a black limousine parked nearby
Bush said his piece into the microphone for CNN. Fox News. He
sympathized with Cindy Sheehan but he wasn't getting out of Iraq.
Crude oil prices on the New York Mercantile Exchange hit $66 a
barrel in trading. The Justice Department concluded that the Penta-
gon has the authority to move National Guard units without the
consent of state governors. The Perseid meteor shower peaked. A man
in Branson, Missouri changed his name to the pronoun "they." A
mother had her forehead tattooed with the web address of a gambling
site after auctioning off advertising space on her head to pay for her
son's school fees. A dog found a baby in a forest south of Nairobi and
took the infant by his swaddling clothes and carried it across a busy
road and through a barbed wire fence and placed it close to her own
puppies. Wal-Mart used an odd civil law to seek $150 in damages
from an Oregon couple who forgot to pay for $10 worth of manure.
A woman emerged from a restaurant in Jacksonville, Florida, into 95-
degree heat and gleefully exclaimed "All right, let's go shopping!"

The night I dropped Shakespeare on the cat the cat was hiding
under four sheets of a weekly taped together with masking tape. The
cat likes to hide under the paper. If you roll a ping pong ball through
a tunnel in the paper when the paper is all bunched up the cat likes to
bat the ping pong ball back out again. He does this every time like a
soccer goalie. Ball rolls in. Ball gets thwacked out. If you take a stick
with a plume on the end and slide it under the paper the cat will claw
at it catch it and tug it and bite it and wrestle with it. The cat really
likes it under the paper which occasionally catches my attention as it
is covered with ads advertising the sexual favors of women. Victoria,
Jasmine, Miranda, Kristy, Gigi, and Nikki. Mistress Matisse.
Transexual Naomi. Governor Escorts. Lisa, Katie, Celeste. Bambi,

Veronica, Candi. Ultimate erotic secrets. College babes. Specialty Videos. Personal touch. Afternoon delight. Hot New Girls. Young Bombshells Ready & Willing. Women with their butts exposed women bending low to emphasize a stupendous cleavage. All in all a remarkably lurid merchandising of sex. Like a pizza delivery. Sex delivered to your home. Warm curves. Young & sassy. Hot & nasty. Like a pepperoni pizza.

The night I dropped Shakespeare on the cat we had watched *Julius Caesar* with Louis Calhern and Caesar, James Mason as Brutus, John Gielgud as Cassius, and Marlon Brando as Mark Antony looking buff and young and fiercely compelling. For the first time I finally got it finally understood why these guys had to kill Caesar. I can't believe I was that dense. It's so obvious. Caesar is about to be crowned dictator for life. How frightening how repugnant that would be to a group of peers. Particularly when you know how mortal this man really is. How given to whims and appetites. So when the film was over I had to get my big edition of Shakespeare out. The Riverside Shakespeare with a sixteenth-century embroidered valance for the cover illustration front and back a courtier in doublet and hose inviting a woman in a pink velvet gown to dance as a fox prances by between them and a large snail sits curiously just behind the woman. This is a heavy book. I would not bring it out except for a special reason. Which in this case was Cassius' speech in scene II act I. Which is an amazing speech underscoring the mortality of Caesar. The language is so completely alive. So wonderfully fresh and turbulent. "The torrent roar'd," says Cassius "and we did buffet it/ With lusty sinews, throwing it aside/ And stemming it with hearts of controversy." That's marvelous, that phrase. "Hearts of controversy." What a wonderfully imagined scene. I had to dive into it again and again. But I grabbed the book from the shelf with too much eagerness. My grip wasn't yet made firm and so the book slipped from my hand and tumbled to the floor. Fell on the cat. Fell on Victoria, Jasmine, Miranda, Kristy, Gigi, and Nikki. Fell on Mistress Matisse. Crushed Transexual Naomi. Crumpled Celeste. Demolished Bambi. Pulverized Candi. And the cat? The cat wasn't there. The cat had slipped out without my knowing.

➤

Thank goodness for the cat. The stealth of the cat. The prudence of the cat. The changeable fidgety cat.

The night I thought I dropped Shakespeare on the cat I felt the reprieve of the man who accidentally goes through a red light without getting hit, the relief of the man who falls from a high cliff only to discover he's been dreaming. But the relief isn't immediate. It takes a little time. There are those few seconds in which the reality of the bed and sheets and room penetrate and so permeate the dream-ridden brain that the dream finally dissipates, melts back into the night from whence it came. There was no cliff, although the fiction of falling, the dream of falling was so real the brain believed all the whirling and twirling and limbs splaying and ground coming up were real. Meaning there is sometimes reality in irreality. Meaning a dream can be mud. Genuine as rain. The space in which I believed there to be a cat and there was no cat was that delicious space we call a fiction. As when a word doubles for something not actually present. Something not present that feels real. But what then is the essential difference between a belief and an actuality? If the emotion is real isn't the fiction real? Real in some sense? In some sense wet and actual, like a tongue? As real as Jasmine and Candi and Mistress Matisse? As real as Caesar? As real as Bush? Is Bush real? The things he says are not real. But there are those who believe it is real. So where is that line? The line between expectation and proof? Between rainbows and algebra? Resin and reason? Paradigm and paradise? The night I thought I dropped Shakespeare on the cat was a night like any other night with one essential difference. There was no cat where I believed there to be a cat. So that the truth was crooked. Not a lie, but a cockeyed truth. Not a lie, but a firmament of gross assumption. A junction between truth and falsehood. A present absence. An absent presence. A fiction. A fiction I dropped on the cat. A reality I dropped on the cat. Who wasn't there. Who was elsewhere. Where fictions do happen. And Shakespeare has a life.

THE MYSTERY OF GROCERY CARTS

I am sitting in the car reading Russell Edson. It's raining heavily.
Roberta has gone into the grocery store for whipped cream and
lettuce. The car is parked in a large parking lot. Water flows down the
windshield in blurry sheets through which I can barely make out the
red neon sign across Queen Anne Avenue North that says Hot Subs
Elliott Bay Pizza Company. A man in a blue shirt gets into a blue
Dodge and drives away. A younger man in a green Volkswagen Rabbit
with a crushed left fender takes his place. A man walks past with a
cigarette dangling from his lower lip and I wonder how he has man-
aged to keep the cigarette going all this way in such heavy rain. He is
almost finished with it. He stubs it out and goes into the grocery
store. I look to the left and notice beads of water dripping from the
wires of the grocery cart. Wait a minute. Are they wires or rods? Is
there a word for that particular part of the grocery cart anatomy?
Would they more properly be described as bars? Crosspieces?
Crossbars? Meshwork? Webwork? Reticulum? I suddenly realize how
arbitrary and limited language can be. The inability to describe the
framework of a grocery cart, or the way the water descends the
windshield, or the contrast between the poplars wavering in front of a
gray sky, the acutely delineated branches of the poplars against the
amorphous gray of the sky, which isn't actually gray, but more of an
opalescent off-white, with here and there deepening areas of gray that
diffuse into the white. Perhaps I could say the sky holds the garrulity
of milk in its murmur of rain and oxygen. The meat of the air sings
to the mud of the earth and as the rain splatters against the glass of
the windshield the emotional life of the sky describes itself as a
rubber band of deep silence stretching into the galaxies in which the
gentle truth of apple blossoms are invented in troughs of promiscu-
ous ambiguity. But none of this solves the true problem at hand
which is what to call the rods or wires on the framework of a grocery
cart. And when did the grocery cart first enter human history. Did the
Sumerians use grocery carts? Did the Babylonians use grocery carts?
Is the grocery cart an adjunct of the automobile? Do the nomads of

Mauritania long to push grocery carts? Why do so many grocery carts find themselves lying in creeks and culverts and roadside ditches? Where are grocery carts produced? Is there a city known for its production of grocery carts? Is there a Detroit of grocery carts? Roberta returns to the car with whipped cream and lettuce and a bunch of other stuff. "Where to now," I say. "Let's go to the video store," she answers. I start the car and we leave. I say nothing about grocery carts. I decide to leave the mystery of grocery carts alone for a while. My thoughts turn instead to the complexities of driving, and the fathomless mystery of gas, and combustion, and what movie to rent, and the harsh yet wonderful glow of taillights in spring rain.

OUR FEELINGS REACH OUT
BEYOND US

In AA they call it "future tripping." Montaigne quotes Seneca: "A soul anxious about the future is most vulnerable." So you have to ask yourself "What am I worried about? Illness? Bankruptcy? Failure? Estrangement? Disapproval? Death? Money? Liquidation?" It is a good question, but the wrong question. The real question is: what is a feeling? Because whatever breathes sense and sensation into us makes us alive. And that encompasses an infinite number of things at any given moment. Gears, necessities, conjurations. Sagebrush, sandpaper, moonlight. For the song is most alive when it turns scarlet as a noon on Mars, which is how a sense of oneself might be extended. Extended forever. And this is what makes iron feel so irredeemably iron, or an angel appear in a bowl of soup.

Think of a current and how that current might be expressed on the surface of a river. Dimples, whirls, rills and folds. Words, wrinkles, commas and meaning. A push in the right direction can make it all chemical. Fluid as thought. An egg hatching into a boulevard, a wisp of incense curling and turning in a slow portrayal of thought. Breath moving and filling words. Words which connect us to the past. Words which connect us to the future. Words which connect us to the present.

We do not begin to take our enjoyment of coffee seriously until we realize we are alive to taste it. This realization can occur as suddenly as tar to the roll of a tire. It is an awareness so big and warm it seems eccentric, outside the realm of the quotidian. But it is exactly that, the quotidian, in which we live. The future is born in the quotidian. In the wine of its whimsy. In the milk of its innocence. In the bones of its transgressions. The movement of grain when the wind moves through it, Shelley's shadow of some unseen Power floating though unseen among us, visiting this various world with as inconstant wing as summer winds that creep from flower to flower, stalk to stalk, seed to steed, stone to stone.   ➔

There are an infinite number of ways to perceive the truth of death. Some of them are chemically lyrical, and some are elemental, a bold vibrato holding a note for a full three minutes, or the folding of cloth napkins in a posh restaurant. Sometimes stumbling into things in the dark can spur feelings of divination, of cosmic inference. Give rise to a notion that whatever form the surf takes pounding the sand might be a hissing revelation of the universe itself in a splay of eternal speculation.

In the very north of North Dakota is a glacial moraine in the shape of an oval part of which extends into Canada. It is this emblem of extension that lights a feeling in the mind of letters extending from this life to the next, as if the mind were a moraine of alphabets deposited by the dead, the dead still living, the dead in their rawhide and bells. The Sioux and the Pawnee and Kiowa and Cheyenne danced them into recognition.

Now think of a tuba, and a large jolly man playing that tuba. There is no frontier for this image but your own ability to cross the border of the familiar to the unfamiliar, the unseen to the seen. The unheard to the herd of elk in its silence in the hills. There is about a piece of toast even a sense of the sacred, or a canvas painted by Rothko, whose fields of color emanate an aura of otherworldly charm. So begins our personal boulevard, our alphabet of shivering presences, the glow of instruments at night in a cockpit guiding us homeward, or the dark and pungent smells of a cellar offering us passage to subterranean events, the phenomenon of quiet gracing the meat in its postponed decay.

The acacia becomes acute when its ache is actuated in our personal soil. How is it possible so many forms can find the rhythm of the literal in the lineaments of the unknown? I feel elastic when those whispers that elevate devotion stir the incense in the air. The mountain is extended in mantles of cloud, though the clouds themselves are wraiths of drifting consciousness. Divine moments of idleness. Everything is alive. Everything craves melody and design. Doorknobs are valentines for the hand. A clump of Dakota dirt is a mystery so warm in the mind it breathes outwardly into our existence the potential of its regenerative essence.

At four o'clock in the morning the scent of sage is pungent, plangent with dawn. The sorcery of words creates a wrinkle in time. The sweetness of expectancy unfolds dragonflies of sedulous desire, equations veined with magnetism and light.

Look over there: there is a claw of mist holding the sky in its palm. And now while it begins to rain the odors reveal the language of meat, a conflict scoured clean as morning. Clay squeezed through the fingers.

Each time I say I a litany of pronouns begins to burn in a map of comical references, each one desperate for the density of the actual. How large is your enjoyment of things? The nectar of definition betrays a tragic adhesion to tense. Present, past, future, pluperfect, subjunctive. As if time and space could be organized in words. Or a trip to Boston explained in a series of coherent events. Which part of the mannequin has been recently moved and which part of the man-nequin evinces the potential of autonomy? An autonomous move, an autonomous sensuality. Here begins a fiction. Here the mind begins to imagine itself assuming the conditions and circumstances of the inorganic, and wonder if that division, too, might be the arbitrary circumstance of language. Exactly how does a silkworm make silk?

The silkworm is not a worm but a moth. The silk from the silk-worm's cocoon is a single, continuous thread. It is made of a protein that is secreted from two salivary glands in the caterpillar's head. What writer does not do the same? What writer does not produce lines, a single continuous line, or lines broken into sentences, so that a paragraph might form, a paragraph that is a form of cocoon, in which the moth of a thought might evolve into a body of words to be issued from the mouth? A body of scintillating words, smooth, lustrous, exquisite as sunlight, the emergence of a meaning whose charge has the fast diffusions of illumination and the soft folds of fabric warming and repudiating the flesh.

What is all this writing for if not a buggy rattling down a dirt road? An image raw and spontaneous as anything Pollock dripped in his atelier, a rattling reality crossing the hill into a landscape of pure invention.

→

Can you sense it? Surmise it? Hazard a guess? Down in some cave of the Paleolithic past feelings whose content remains disturbing and enigmatic are translated into vision as a fire dances its shapes and shadows on the cavern wall. That's where it all started. Here is where it continues. Some irritant or another extended and expanded by language until it is fenced in like a large and anxious dog, its tongue out in a drool of suspicion, a pair of eyes peering from behind those protective slats, a low growl of warning dilating the moment to pure distinction.

Open your mouth, hemorrhage knots, radiant clusters of sound. They will penetrate the gloom of ignorance like a lighthouse penetrating the dark on the coast of some northern country whose rugged shores chasten the slop of the ocean. It remains a mystery to me why people enjoy golf. Those oysters of sincerity we dig up in the night are so much more entrancing, engaging, like a telescope sticking its nose in the stars. Each word is a conjuration of creosote, a distillation whose tarry glop preserves images of rail and railroad tie, pole upon pole upon pole on the prairie, or thickets of Pennsylvania. You see how easy it is to stretch a feeling into meringue, a medium like worm-wood, and watch as thoughts and figurations bubble up through it, forming sunflowers and personality, or a soft red opening for a fat, juicy strawberry. This is why religion is always so magnetic and cumbersome, like public utilities. This ecstatic life of morals shaped and broken comes together in Spanish, or Latin, or German or English, and a purity of thought which cannot be bottled or bought finds its amaryllis and clarity in thunder at midnight.

A story does more than tolerate its own narration. It also moves objects forward. Topics for discussion. Each life is a safari, a pilgrimage, a bullfrog sitting on a rock preparing to leap into the stream and be carried wherever the stream might take it. There is nothing more sudden or awkward or wonderful than the touch of someone else's skin. There is, for instance, an animal coming out of my thumb, a head, a mind, an ecstasy of limb and ligament seeking a syntax of contour and bone, a forkful of rain and a thought glistening in language freshly plucked from the sky. There is a frontier of emotion that begins with dialect and proceeds with banners. Three kinds of acrobatics incriminate gravity but only one kind of cake can hold itself together in so much sugar, and that is an elegance so literal it resembles silverware.

I feel tangled in the realism of elm. Yet bundles of air enshrine the poem in rubies. This is because there is no single feeling but many feelings. There can be an octopus slithering among rocks. But there can also be a neon sign somewhere in Kansas bleeding its blues and yellows and reds into the night air. I despise the triteness of people who say the night sky makes them feel small. The night sky makes me feel huge, and exalted, the way it should. You are not separate from these things you are a part of these things. The sound of a harpsichord is sharp as a razor. But this isn't because of skin and nerves and hollows and convolutions in your head. This is because sound is organized in the warm dark soil of the soul. This is because the stars on Orion's belt lodge a fresh pizzicato in the gardens of eternity.

Photographs are cruel. They remind us that destiny is not fixed but open to an undetermined future of infinite possibilities and limitless scope. Nervous crows on a railroad track. Miners in the Yukon 1899. Cowboys herding cattle. President Lincoln at Gettysburg. Black man's hands grasping space. Ballerina sitting in a corner, her legs splayed. Rumanian girl herding sheep in the fog. Bearded man shot from beneath reaching high to attach a rope to a cable descending from a helicopter the fuzz of his beard sticking out contrasting with the lucidity of the rope and the blur of the helicopter blades.

Eyes penetrate through the film to the future. Which is now the present. Which is now the past. Which is now an emotion. A fever. An impulse. An amperage. A delicious yaw. An alley in Panama absolved from its fate in an alchemy of quarreling light.

We end with an essence we do not begin with an essence. We are our own ghosts. We haunt ourselves. We grow into our shoulders hoping for wings and find in our throats a wallet of weight and currency. The seductions of communion, the heat and light of a welding torch, the meaning of blue or the sound of a guitar in a fourteenth century castle. There is nothing so ineffable as the scent of infinity, the varnish on a groan, the diamonds on a windshield diffracting the

➤

sun. Nothing so sublime as the heartbeat in a dog. A raft of giraffes moving down an African river, or big blue dahlias placed lovingly and strategically around the body of a dead raccoon. The purpose eludes us, but the beauty includes us, and the machinery of writing begins to dream itself into a continuous expansion, a rumble, a roar, a man disappearing over the horizon on a tongue of asphalt.

PHILIP LIVES:
A LAMENT FOR LAMANTIA

Philip is gone. Philip is dead. Long live Philip.

Philip lived and breathed poetry. He called poetry a miracle in words. Which is precisely what it is. A miracle in words. Rhapsodes of pain passionate wavelengths tortured minerals sublimated into bubbling autonomy. Delicious anomalies paradisiacal pancakes morning prayer in the bowl of dawn. Fireworks in Mexican villages. The aroma of dragons. Analogues parallels pantisocratic parakeets.

Piles of sawdust on the workshop floor. An errant chorus in a stick of sequence. Fragments of meaning utopian as towels and metaphysical as a sheepskin rug.

If anyone refers to this as word play I will punch them in the nose. Surrealism is not word play surrealism is a mouthful of light a towering urge to mangle the language beat it into tungsten a raging river fastened to the hood of a jeep old clocks yawning in oysters oracular ore at the core of an oar a Martian umbrella dressed in music.

Philip was a regular at the eternal smorgasbord of mood and penumbra. He astonished us all with his granite balloons his sensations and hurry his addiction to talking his elevators and hardware his opinions and theories his immense curiosity his ceaseless thermos of romantic green tea. His beads his buds his beans his occasional beards.

A lament is sad but this isn't sad this is a black emotion pinned to a crimson grammar this is a feeling in the form of a needle a basketball of glass a thought made of ribbon a jar of headlights a Tuesday varnished with sonnet milk the smell of popcorn in a theatre lobby the month of July split open to reveal topaz trout swimming in a sewing box a city of toads and charming absorptions desperado poets beating on a gong a phantom hammerhead walking around in its previous bones.

He reminded me a little of Peter Lorre he could talk for hours emitting a reddish glow of crocodiles and ethereal escalators a poetry of X-rays and telepathic plumage a piece of weather reflected in the sheen of ocean sand fairyland teeming with diamonds the convulsive variety of curbs in Pakistan the anatomy of any flavor sunspots radio waves crackling the rumble of palominos on Colorado dirt.

He would enter a state of rapture and tell you poetry is not a palliative but a provocation. That we live in a subterranean homesick world. That the beauty of a rattlesnake is an astonishing thing. That the rattle of the rattlesnake shows philosophy and taste.

One afternoon he got tangled in the seatbelt of our Subaru and kept right on talking vivid as a medieval illumination struggling to get out of the material world.

He had a fever for the marvelous for photosynthesis and caves for Matisse for Magritte for a can of cantatas. For the Dada jackpot of a chemical railroad sizzling in a cast iron frying pan. For banjos and balusters and bandaged horizons nostalgic as nudes for syllables for solder and jackknives for acetylene sardines liquid oxygen seasoned with thyme for a woman's gaze drowning in gauze for being and nothingness infinity plunged in clouds a camel squeezed through the eye of a needle Rimbaud walking the streets of Harar the quality of light in a stained glass window a silver watch hemorrhaging mohair the immensely deliciously ineffable thrill of saying the unsayable without being able to say it. For bookstores embroidered with alleys for the pathology of crosswalks for knowledge coined in the halls of cranberry for torque for torsion for incidental light for the Big Bang exploding out of Mallarme's fan for the mocha machinery of eighteenth century Ecuador for the guts of a word stuck in somebody's ear for wool for outmaneuvering burlap for unpacking a suitcase of swords and kettledrums and smokestack lightning.

Dear Philip thank you for the legacy. For the consonants orbiting a vowel. For the axles and gears of magnetic tiaras greased by incantation. For the extraordinary ordinariness of a wheelbarrow burdened with the lung of a Sumerian pronoun. For the elevator paneled with insect wings. For the batch of words baked in eucalyptus and polished with Deadwood, South Dakota. For the hypodermic feeling of a resplendent opinion pinned to my lip. For writing wild and writing a wilderness. For a sense of history swimming with music. For teaching me that poetry is necessary and cruel because it is the first thing in the world to come alive. For being alive. For thrusting your tongue into a pubis of loam and telling us what it tasted like. For the many prepositions surgically removed from a jukebox. For your hat of shoals and Shasta pollen. For your crystal rails and volcanic sunsets.

What apparel best suits these sentiments? How shall I dress to say a final farewell to you?

Words with shiny black exoskeletons and watercolor birds. A gem with a head. A life on the brink. Geometric odors flaring in the siroccos of my unmitigated hat.

Missoula

for Andrew Joron

You go to Missoula, Montana, to do a poetry reading. You have been invited to read there by someone you have never met. A friend from San Francisco will also be there. You believe this will be a good occasion for a road trip. For you and your wife. Maybe someone will buy some books. Various reasons for going there seep into your consciousness and crowd out the purest of all reasons for going there which is the joy of momentum.

Extension. Expansion. Range.

The hum of the hymn of the hum of the road.

You get in the car and drive out of Seattle. It's early April and raining heavily. The city thins. Trees thicken. The rain lets up. You can stretch. You can breathe. The country is open so the mind itself opens. Leaves agitated, flapping, flickering tell you what is in the air. River tattooed with irritant whirling. Cottonwood at the frontier of perception. Language cut in half hemorrhaging metaphors. This shows that thread is red and insight is blue. The anatomy of morning smelling of rain and strawberries. The slow drool of light over the edge of a mountain.

You stop in North Bend for breakfast at the Twin Peaks Café.

What exactly is asphalt, you wonder. What are the components of asphalt? Asphalt is the cupcake of confrontation. Asphalt is nobody's fault. Asphalt is for brawling. The brawl of wheels. The brawn of wheels.

Gravel is anything. The gravel just shrugs.

You order pancakes with a side order of bacon, large glass of orange juice, and a cup of coffee. Your wife orders a spinach omelet. Blood flows more freely when the body has food in it. Apples shine brighter. Objects yell at the window. Let us out. Let us in. Let us remedy space with linen and thread. Let us conjure your nerves into the glamour of composition. The management of wheels. The politics of gray and the squirrels of inquiry. Unleash articulation. Attire the morning with Wurlitzer chrome.

Life is an amalgam, you think, an accumulation of moments, sensations, perceptions, thoughts, reflections that turn into memory, turn into cantos and coal.

Become conundrum and backbone. The slow diameter of ketchup. The insurgency of skin.

You see hawks, horses grazing, their necks in a graceful descent, their soft muzzles working the grass, blue rag tied to a fence post, a house sitting alone with a jumble of junked machinery scattered on the grounds. Everything in a reverie of the west.

You stop for gas in Vantage, which is a tiny town with a museum of petrified gingko overlooking the Columbia River gorge. It's a great place to stop and get gas and wonder what direction your life is going in. You look for a gingko and a picnic table where you once had a picnic with your father a few years before he died. A young man arrives in a pickup. He is wearing a cowboy hat. Out here, you realize, men wear cowboy hats. It's exciting to be in a part of the country where men wear cowboy hats. Though not too keen to be in a part of the country where they might also be inclined to vote for Bush and believe the world was slapped together in six days by a slaphappy God.

Albeit, out here, you cannot deny it. Religion is everywhere. It is in the rocks. The aridity. The smell of sage. The blacktop. Sunsets inscribed in reveries of grain. Glossaries of dirt. Invocations of hop. Pallet of pears lifted by chain. Paper on a table soft as an afterthought. Birds knotted in confluent air. Mornings bulging with goldenrod.

In the beginning was the Logos; the Logos was with God and the Logos was God. He was with God in the beginning. Through him all things came into being, nothing that exists came into being apart from him. In him was Life, and this life was the Light of men. The Light shines on in the darkness, and the darkness has never conquered it.

Can there be anything more Gothic than a field of lava caked and brittle since the Pleistocene? Here in oblivion bowling is a daydream. A thin piece of buzz. The savage claw of conviction.

Words pop into your mind: vellum Valium enamel. Nice combination, that. Maybe you can use it in a poem sometime.

You look around and see de Kooning colors everywhere. Warm earth tones. Beige, ocher, brown. Tan, leather, olive. If you had some time you could coat some narrative on that barn over there. Give it a life. A life of fiction. A life of fiction starring Sam Shepard and Penelope Cruz. A life full of buckskin, catastrophe, and rickety pickups. A life of ease. A life of storms. A life of booze.

You think about words. You think about words all the time. Thinking about words is engrossing. Thinking about words humors the candy of alternation. You love to do it. You do it all the time. You bead consonants with vowels. You make hats out of borscht. You permit the truth of peppermint to gurgle the vastness of chalk. You put words in your head and light them with thought. Let them idle on the alchemy of paper. Bundle them in grammar. Hurt them into speech.

The word 'lid,' you decide, has an aggressive logic. But you don't know why the word 'lid' is suddenly in your head. You picture your head with a lid on it. You lift the lid and bats fly out.

When it comes to writing poetry you can be diligent or cryptic. Or both. You can be diligently cryptic or cryptically diligent.

You think of handling pain like a yoyo. Pain on a string. Going up and down. Picture that. Mental or physical pain. On a string. Going up and down.

You get back on the road and see many wonderful and lonely things. A chair sitting in a yard, all by itself. Meadows, roads, gullies, hills. American flags in front of house trailers. Bluebells in a ditch. Two men in an aluminum boat in the middle of Moses Lake. A bold blob of oak coming into greater and greater definition. Junked cars. Sage and grain elevators and high rolling hills. Rivers, ponds, marshes, lakes. A garden of heliotrope and amaryllis. Cows licking cubes of salt. Cottonwood on the banks of the Yakima River.

Dirt everywhere in furrows, rills, crests. It's planting season. There are tractors everywhere stirring up dust. It's a hard life out here.

A hard life to work the dirt and put seeds in it and hope they come up and stay up until it's time to harvest whatever it is you put in the dirt and watered and tended.

Hours later you arrive in Missoula. You arrive in Missoula to read poetry.

Why, you wonder, why am I here in Missoula to read poetry when the life out here is so hard? So desolate. So down-to-earth. So resigned.

You are approaching your 60s. You have devoted your entire life to words. To putting words together. Why?

Because elements and minerals. Because apples and nebulae in outer space. Because sand is no secret and dust is the opposite of popcorn. Because linoleum is consonant with sweat. Because society is always trying in some way or other to grind us down to a single flat surface. Because reality is crushed by mesmerizing sounds. Because cellophane is silly and pleasure rolls in waves through the body. Because moods seep into the skull and congeal into lagoons like candy in a library. Because the biology of the trumpet occasions valves. Because the divinity of metal awakens the machinery of flight. Because the rain is wet and the memory is warm. Because birds are alert and nervous and the complexities of human biology become more taxing with age. Because excursion compounds the rapture of words and the rapture of words is ravenous for excursion. Because poetry approximates the temperature at the core of the sun and the evidence of stone is inscrutable when one's dreams are red. Because the smell of a cellar. Because towers in the distance. Because goblets, camellias, menus, and poles. Because space continually expands. Because heat is wonderful. Because razors and cork and eyebrows and lamps. Because words are everywhere and obstinate as salmon.

Because here you are. Here you are in Missoula.

GERTRUDE STEIN AGAIN AND AGAIN

Gertrude Stein said a sentence is this. This which is partly a feeling
and partly a physiology. This is better than stirred. This is angora.
This is why insects do not have bones. Insects have wings. Insects have
smears on a windshield. This should be perceptible in pebbles. Every
sentence begins as an insect and ends by supposition. My entire ego is
at stake. I stand here before you naked as a weight. Footsteps on a
hardwood floor. Spit-polished and ready to roar. Anything jangly and
jasper and jelly and jade. Epoxy. Socket. Volt. Worlds of words rife
with perpetual reverie. A sentence might build an intestine and then
anchor itself in a radio where it is obvious a voice is coming out of it
in delicate neons. Choose a hue and go to Las Vegas. In spite of a
sentence is to say so and crown the reptile with rope and palpitation.
This is an indication that books are exultant. And perhaps a little
surreal. Like the anatomy of summer. A poem is partly a pasty within
itself. A part of a poem may be a sentence while other parts thicken
into mallets without any meaning. A sentence is made by balancing a
remark on top of a spine. The very sky begins to occur in butter. The
lucidity of a Vermeer. Make an alphabet bear thunder and you will
arrive at the roots of life as slowly as it takes a stalk of celery to grow
into a placenta of snow. It is not in the nature of a metaphor to dis-
place rubber with logical development. Different sounds are required
to become a simile sinking to the bottom of the mind like night when
it percolates through the skull of day and spreads itself on the bread
of oblivion. Water is wide. Black shapes balanced in personality. Eye-
balls and membranous folds in the larynx. Daybreak in a bayou. The
difference between a pancake and a waffle is small pools of syrup. It
takes a sentence to say the cutlery must be arranged according to
strict codes of etiquette but it takes a balcony of bone to raise a jujube
into opera. Sometimes a trip to the bank will help clarify things.
There is an energy there that feels like rules aroused into shape.
Poetry when it is a shaft around which something turns. Poetry read
in a hot room in Portland. You can electrify yourself with an emotion
so big it has forecasts. Grammar is perfectly understandable. A

machine in its skin of words. Various hues begin to traffic in jasmine. It is the sentence that crawls off the page to become three hundred gallons of Tuesday.

A TRIP TO THE LIBRARY

The shock dealt to the Aristotelian world view could not have been greater had the stars bent down and whispered in the astronaut's ears. Clearly, there was something new, not only under the sun, but beyond it. We could feel it in the air. We could feel it in the clocks, and taste it in the architecture of our intercourse. We could feel it in the C-clamp, and the philosophy surrounding the use of the C-clamp. But what was it?

We rotated our arms until the library opened. The ghosts of Aksum were everywhere. They appeared in a girl's braids that ran in tight rows over the crown of her head and ended in an explosion of curls, echoing the hairstyles on ceramic Aksumite heads. They were in the clay water jug an old woman carried behind her back, tied with a leather rope slung low around her shoulders.

Distress was apparent in the clams. They churned in the sand like belly dancers, exciting sentiments of rightness and fondue. A piece of chlorophyll evolved a luminous sleeve of popcorn and gold. Immense opportunities glistened in my leg.

Mating in the open is risky, but reading temperatures rise surrounded by so many shelves. There were books everywhere. Books within books. Books in brooks and sermons in stones. Experiences of mint and idea, coulombs and eggs. Fiddles and combs. Spiritual curls and empirical necessities. Mosaics. Jewels. Clay bells and beckoning memorandums.

I noticed a circle form a bezel set with diamonds.

"Don't be afraid," said Singh, "the radius won't bite." This is because the circumferences are seasonal. They imitate money in the spring, turning hard and metallic, exhibiting presidents on one side, monuments on the other.

Alternative transportation is provided in the form of current events. The higher you travel, the less there is. No trees. No telephones. What remains is the immensity of the sky, gaunt slopes scrubby with thistles and wild grasses, the roar of glacial torrents in dark ravines, and the powerful pull of the first gods ever feared by men.

Not much is quieter than falling snow. But sometimes turning a page can sound more like wisdom than a hearing aid.

Guano might be translated as auricula, or infinite implication.

Runners appear carrying ancient ideas. They hang from the mouth invisible and salt.

A bell rings. The Arctic Circle is gathering for a dance. The upright piano was positioned at center stage, bathed in light. The music made us a boat and we mingled with birds, and the tall sounds of the Aleutians, until it was time to leave.

As we exit the library we see the beauty of being hearty and theoretical. There is an advantage to secreting things like neon the average person doesn't understand. When the wickiup wakes up, the cutlery outlines cake and the technology of appetite.

Ruby's hopes of winning a Nobel Prize rested on a conception of wax that was simply riveting.

Outside, the air was crisp and tautological. Everybody seemed a little confused about what to do next. Like the pop-up silhouettes on a police firing range, uncertainties such as this represent not only what is but what might be. As quantum physics sees it, every "real" particle is surrounded by a corona of virtual particles and antiparticles that bubble up out of the vacuum, interact with one another, and then vanish, having lived on borrowed, Heisenberg time. Affinities among words create new life, then gamble on khaki. This is the way of the universe. Tongues wag and cities are born. Music brings literature, literature brings Houyhnhnms and wing nuts and libraries emerge from the ground, plump, itchy, and wet, crashing through our lives like unrelenting paragraphs. Climates of thought considered as ink. Words immersed in milk. Milk immersed in stars. Oblivion everywhere blazing bucking and black.

AESOPIAN SMELT

A poetry that can coin lamps has little to do with needles. It sprays fish allegory and a flea. It is meat and muscle. It is obviously allspice. It would smirk at jodhpurs if jodhpurs were oak. It radiates eyes. It is a poetry of darkness and burning wicks and begonia ooze. The flank it timbers is epicurean with conviction. Words come falling down to fill the scrotum with French. Physics in a bag. The fabric of analogy, which is silk and rawhide. Autumn is a habit with jeans. Words are always biochemical, an extreme olive they permeate with ballast. The fantasia of a hand which is a mood, a kind of ambergris. All radar is rich in the obliquity of hair. The near cream of our neighbors is rendered neutral by the savor of our fervid handstands. A jaw and a brother are soon Missouri. The hills are maneuvered by wind. All underwater daylight fragments Halloween. Even the trees creak with hydrogen. Can you think critically? Can you lift a jade monkey? Homogeneous magnetic bagels issued photographs of a single viola. Such were the stars. Such were wet and flint. A shadow obtruded from jumping alchemical facts by the horse. A syntax for toast a beard for the almond. A black fact is a white jingle. Sound is often painted to be near the fiber of an odor. The smell of trout, for instance, or the certification of chisels. Oil you and teaspoon flannel. I will volt you agility on the bottle. Yes, sir, and Muddy Waters in a rhapsody of emissions. Pump the nod from your neck, then cement the moonlight in long smooth clouds. Sunday has beached. Absorb the parrot. There is more to a world than tone. There are also words. And amalgams of logic forming biochemical suggestions.

A BIG NOISE

Let's make a great big noise. Everything is boiling, sparkling, splattering and bright. Everything is henna. Everything is marble. Everything is the name of a cat or the name of a city or the name of a decade.

Life flowers into rhythm at the window of drums.

The song of the prepositions melts in my mouth. At, on, under, around, in, out, from, about. All melt into one large mass of prepositional pudding. All spatial reference tastes suddenly of tapioca.

I ripen into a lamp of Sumerian oil.

I tumble into the street translucent and lavish, a ball of veins.

This is not a joke I'm not kidding. I mean it.

An angel bounces me to Tacoma. I become a railroad engineer. I write poems at the head of the train all the way to Los Angeles.

And in the morning I open my eyes.

I see a mouth of gold vomiting reeds and shadows.

I see a British heartache moaning like a hatchery of bells.

I see a cat sobbing radios.

I see a mind revel in glue.

I see a museum of ice melt into shoulders and the wild anatomy of laundry.

I believe, as did the Blackfeet and Crow, that thunder and wind are caused by the flapping of a giant bird that lives in the mountains.

Give me rhythm.

Give me temperature and arteries.

Give me a sound that incorporates cloth.

Give me a liquid sound that crowns the intuition of irises.

Give me the hot dry noise of an armadillo's dream.

There is a description of the landscape I like very much as it supplements our knowledge of plants and canals.

The delicious vertigo of foreign cities. Bratislava. Changchun.

It is the poet's responsibility, among other things, to tend to the animals. To feed them. To help them propagate. The houses are turned upside down by enormous birds. The poet must encourage this. The women are too well dressed. ➤

The man who sawed himself in half gave new life to the print wheel.

Rhymes and measures obscure the ores of Ecuador.

Rhymes and measures dim the lights of Rangoon.

Praise be to a woman's hips.

Magic is the engine of youth.

The lumber of heaven is the fortification of old age.

Moo goo gai pan.

The moon is sifted through the breath and issues from a ring of lips.

MENISCUS

The flamboyance of trout awakens the cadence of water. It is a symptom of birch. Piano and rocking chair confirm the belt of Orion. The fungus did to the salami what the salami did to the harmonics of fable. It became a scrap of royalty, an amaryllis by the bay. Everything turned quiet as a mountain trumpet. Precision was whatever conviction proved most elastic. A candle above the palette moved a kilowatt of line along a surface of paper. A lesion of circumstance gave us a peak at future provocations. We decided to mow the lawn. Later, we chose which spoon to use for the ice cream with an ease neither of us had felt before. Was it our eccentricity, a frivolous ablution, or something even more fugitive, like a fugue? Eternity, you said, is more than a proverb. It is also a warm breathing, a word at the brim of the mouth about to be pushed into sound. This is how an insinuation begins. You can follow its tracks to the door. Outside, a galaxy wheels above the horizon, slobbering glamour and cold. There is a magnet of love called romance and a syllable with a core of black. This is what makes coagulation so memorable and red. Coats are even effective as violas when the spine churns with meat and wings blast out of the acorns. A tube of snowflakes blows a smooth music toward a fist of morality. The fist unclenches, the fingers blossom into accord, and a parakeet lands on your shoulder. Bullet or area code, you wonder, pondering a book of geometry, all those parallels and circles answering an inward chaos only a scab of music could turn mauve. Most lids demonstrate a little tension when you lift them. But some, like the eyelids, open more slowly to test the diameter of day when the curtain has been abruptly opened. A limestone idea tempted the goshawk closer. A convertible speeding across Pennsylvania brought Duchamp to mind, and that large shattered glass in which a mechanical bride floats, floats to this day, like something personal and raw, a special feather, or a memory whose parts consist of delight and bluebells. Let me ogle you there at the table. You look so marvelous, so wonderful and silly, dressed like a gold mine in darkness and pages of light. Is that a wedding dress, or a sidewalk hemorrhaging dahlias? I have always loved the color pink. If gravity feels heavy, it is not because of the froth bouncing on the surface of the water, but the way it is calculated with rings housed in crystal. Mayonnaise is generally housed in a buxom glass jar. But no vivacity can linger long in such a cell, not without first evincing pleasure, and then shining against a background of ink, like a freshly written sentence. One that whirls, and hits a few wrong notes, just to let us know it is something ill-defined as a dividend, and more like a bell.

POINT-BLANK AND SCRAGGILY

Modal chime of chips of cadence. Vapor pothole. Adobe bleeding a
handsaw. Then stamina. About back. Wicker sometimes. Some made
there the pouring. Compensations are treasure to miracle an intimate
logic. It elicits a toggle bolt. Have is with. By it the arbitrary are breed.
Bosons of voiceover Petrarch. Telescopes because every consequence
glories from a third variety of reed. There is a top of the cabbage that
insinuates rest. On seam. Brabble anyone dance. Way nothing benefit.
Syllables gurgled by an advisor of western perspective and Aristotle.
The innuendo is puckered in Ophiuchus. Cloth ingot. Fork source.
Radius mass. Bought off if. An a because sometimes a the apple. Just
of mud. Off there colleagues sometimes glowing. The nose performs a
deck to believe it to even beckon sense. Dairy simulations. A barrel of
magazines also exposures Plato. All to an in. All to loom a firm jersey
of gossamer violence. A tiny disease that outlines song. A forlorn step
to overcome fiction with a hard lieutenant. Lipstick notwithstanding.
Fat names that writhe in loss like royalty. Heredity hitherto logical
and lurid. Lyceum massage. Meat that models a modal Saturday in
perfect subway cornets. Everything drenched in dark like a dream
freighted with print. Shakespeare with goose bumps. Plato with a
horrendous verve. Seabirds with webbed feet. Quartz that boils
daylight when struck with pennies. A slender red fluid married to a
voice that pulls itself apart with a lever to reveal a violet encrustation
of Welsh.

CASUS BELLI

I live in a great military power. Everybody loves tattoos. Tattoos and guns. Jewelry and guns. Bikinis and guns. Movies with big explosions. Guns.

Ever see a skeleton dance on a flashlight? Everywhere you look you see rattlesnakes of glue and calculus. Tanks rolling over archeological sites. Spasms of daylight dripping the noise of confrontation.

Momentum turning scarlet in a beard of rain.

The jolly old reptile of war kisses our knuckles with bricks. You have to imagine death as a necessary adjunct to life to live here. Otherwise everything would appear to be insane.

The prodigality of rock 'n roll ignites prodigies of shrapnel and light. The delirium of noon is sautéed on a sonnet hemorrhaging chrome. Our idealism is served raw. There are no metaphors for death. It's a mere trigger away. Button on a panel. Word in the wire.

We're always nervous but we like that. We like being on the edge. Daylight balanced on a nerve. Adrenalin is our favorite drug. It's better than Methedrine. It is an extreme candor. The honesty of meat. Scraps of lasagna. A chin falling through its own skin. Jagged bone extending where a hand once wiggled its fingers.

Everything is ravenous for divine intervention. A thunderous heliocentric eyeball to appear in the sky to put an end to it all. Zeus hurling lightning bolts at the enemy. You cannot stop an addiction like this with nuance. You have to be direct. Sympathy is cruel. Existence is fierce. Gold dust blown in the wind. Walter Huston laughing his head off.

Have you ever fired a rifle? Pressed a button and watched something blow up? Killed anyone? Knifed anyone? Pulled a pin on a grenade?

Nothing comes from nothing.

And yet the divine is a voluptuous burden.

Take your clothes off. Walk into the water. How does it feel?

You can't do better than fried chicken and the scent of gunpowder.

When the lights go down our emotions turn infrared. Everything about you, streets, walls, alleys, ambushes, mists, brighten in an ecstasy of fear. When blood wells from a wound you know you're there. Stinging bursts of life in a neck full of fists.

INCLINED

The moment Patsy Cline wraps her voice around your head
it's time.

—Nico Vassilakis

It's time. Time to get crazy. Time to spread the jelly of supposition. Time to build a meaningful duration of sound and fury and call it a day.

Time to go for a midnight walk.

Time to bruise the somnolence of mass with a fist of prayer.

Time to eat the rich. Time to impeach Bush.

Time to identify the meaning of cotton. Because face cream and petroleum jelly are excruciatingly balsamic. And because daylight is new and strange when it assumes the savor of skin.

Time to prove the existence of personality.

Time to be sincere. And bring words together in a sweetness full of flowers and raptures easy to patch together with an umbrella, sewing machine, and 42 gallons of critical density. It is possible here to trace at least three interesting reasons why the importance of a search for a 3° K microwave radiation background was not generally appreciated in the 1950s and early 1960s. First, because direction is a bland word and must be combined with flashlights. Secondly, because the habit of twirling one's thumbs is justified by the absurdity of existence. Third-ly, because refrigerator magnets provoke tarantulas into tarantellas whenever the differentiation of matter into planets and stars makes it easier to introduce the concept of drills and find examples of social extravagance pouring into one's ears like geländesprungs, or brooms.

Meaning it's time. Time to erase all drudgery from the equity of age.

Time to linger in the marvelous drugstores of the future in which pieces of sunlight are incident to the blatant asymmetry of desire.

Time to separate what is necessary from what is unnecessary and curl it around a finger and imagine it as a ring of woodwinds spark-ling with trumpets and bells.

Time to become detached and aloof and deliriously askew.

All that is not prose is furniture. And all that is not furniture is ghostly.

It's all about fucking, observes Mr. Nico Vassilakis of Seattle, Washington.

Go ahead sneeze.

Reverie solicits a road of falseness to get to the truth of mohair. There is enough reality in a tinkling necktie to expand the conjecture of the hinged versus the unhinged into sachets of fragrant bathymetry. Because ambiguities abound in the drive to consider the carpentry of tea. The beauty of refraction is pages and pages of shrewd saturation.

Rapture sprains the gavel. And I fall to pieces.

Sit Anywhere

We are in a cafeteria of the metaphysical. There are spoons. There are
knives. There is ketchup. There is Spinoza and coleslaw. There is
Hegel and doughnuts. There is Swedenborg and jam. Forks and plates
and Formica-topped tables. What happens inside is abstract and
stunning. Everybody gets happy in pecan. Scandinavia trembles in the
coffee. We all turn discursive contemplating pie. Life thickens by the
jukebox. Mysteries grow and die with a 45. We own but our experi-
ences. Everything else is potential, or licensed. Footprints in space
money and Ptolemy au gratin potatoes a copper reverberation.
Eternity and suns and fugues in tubes. A duet in clay, a thick woolen
cloth. An artery after a pulse acquires meaning. A coral beard and a
charbroiled longitude. Rimbaud in a booth with Patti Smith and
Anne Waldman. A language torn into shreds of revelation. An
umbrella and a sewing machine on an operating table. Tennessee cast
in stone. A law full of loops and a loop full of laws. A steamboat pilot
playing Stephen Foster on a violin. It is massive to accept the reality of
the fruit bat or push music into a mosquito. The alloys are allowed to
alloy but the assumptions must stew in character. The logarithm is
simply a mustard for the fierce proportions of a present tense. If the
journey is hard then the writing is indigo. Astronomy matters. It is
constantly asphalt. Ask any highway. Travel any hill. When it rains in
the ocean there is nothing so pertinent as a bucket of ice. Diversity in
barns. Vivacity in meat. Sentences moving thousands of pancakes
toward their destiny as thought. As things to think about. As dough
and pastels. As spoons and inflammation. As the gleam of syrup. As a
pat of butter. As a Copernican spoon holding a diamond in suspen-
ded disbelief. As the crash of plates. As the crash of forks and spoons.
As the crisis of a wounded animal gleaming in its fur. As a freshly
dilated telephone ringing in oblivion. Do you like to watch the stars?
I like to watch the stars. Animals with backbones. Words full of
yearning. That boiling which understands endeavor. It takes years to
understand a cherry. Take twilight. The energy dedicated to cloth.
How does one understand these things? The door that suddenly

opens to a room full of soup. Beautiful soup. Dollars and popcorn.
Trout and eggplant. Discourse cannot be photographed. Because the
words are magnetic and widen into snow. Because the menu is pure
light. Because the tables are made of protons. Because life is patterned
energy. Because the fog is a beautiful silent drum. And the syrup
pours slowly like the dream of a rose.

AN ACCIDENTAL TREATISE
ON THE PARAGRAPH GLANDS
OF GRAVY CANYON

In the discussion of the Mesopotamian writing the observation was made that in certain apologies or piccolos this writing had more of the characteristics of a syllabic than a logographic cheese, or antediluvian antelope. Thus, for instance, the old Akkadian draperies and the Cappadocian trigonometries of the old Assyrian merchants were written to a great extent with syllabic scarves, while the cathedrals of France were described much later as arteries and amplitudes confined to the enzymes of language.

The unwieldy syllabic magnets were used to attract libraries. Each letter exuded a gulf, an abyss or estuary that evoked opium and invisible granaries of Phoenician oat. The derived cuneiform syllabaries are not much different from the movements of the semiotic semen wriggling into the paragraph sack of the Mesopotamian hippopotamus.

What we have now is a frangipani of cuneiform syllabaries all used in company with a more or less limitless number of word casseroles. Bowls of steaming social gist and syllabic zygote developing in the mouth as tissues of excited meaning.

A cuneiform wedge resembles a golf tee, or light emanating from a dark hole in the desert. Semantic elements such as these oscillate between barbershops and petitions for the liberation of desire. These little known theories crackle with inconsistency. However, it should be noted that the proportion of theoretical carp to the actual cartilage of reality is liberally taped with gauze and viscous secretions of prose. The emphasis on fiber is accidental and can make you glad.

The real question is: where did the Semites get the idea of using signs which would indicate the consonants but not the vowels?

Secondly, when does a syllable become a bullet, and when does a vowel become a gland?

Important conclusions can be drawn from a propeller. When the propeller turns, the sentence moves forward stirring material from the bottom of the mind and then veers into the horizon. This may be perceived as a slightly curving line, or mark denoting heaven and Saturday.

The main reason for this assumption is water. In the course of time snow melted and rain fell and became a fetus. If, then, we understand the process of development as a boundary continually expanded into thumbs and ligaments, we can see how Paris might be full of people, and poets like Guillaume Apollinaire.

DUBUFFET BUFFET

Look at your palettes and rags. The slightest irregularities in the thickness of the layers of paint contribute spirit. There is a whole scale of degrees between being and non-being. Go wild. Do not be concerned with theory, but with actuality. The aspect and manner of affixing a color are actually far more important than the choice of the color itself. It is the same with poetry. It's neither the substance of words nor their sound that constitutes their power, but the evocations they trigger.

A painter's basic action is to smear. There is music in oil, being in the movement of our hand. The hand, its impulses, unconscious habits, innate reactions and force offered raw, will awaken forms aswarm with echoes, resonances, and overtones. Splotches, welts, smears and ribbons of paint disperse moods and impressions, a maelstrom of fiery silver, furious pinks, nipples like knobs, glitteriness in running streams. Use purple as you would a welding torch, ocher as you would a rope. Some rusty iron, a muddy road. Put it fat and rubbed and real into your life. Say what you mean and be strong and exultant about it. The slight gaps or intervals caused by scumbling the brush are all exciting and valid, so long as they're alive and delirious.

Fall in love with violence, Coltrane and Bach. Painting is about what we see, what we can see. It requires the highest degree of delirium. Make it all happen with seething amusement. Startle the eyes like a railroad signal, the mirror in the belly of an African fetish.

The distinction between normal and abnormal is false. Who is normal? Are you normal?

Paint upside down. Paint with your feet. Roll on the canvas smeared with blue. Smeared with black. Smeared with fists of madder red.

Each material has its own language and is a language. The skin of a fish or a reptile, a hurricane of line, a color encountered on the street, are just as real and actual as our moods and seasons of the heart. Sticks, trowels, knives, or a heavy impasto with sand say one thing. A spatula or sponge or a shiny piece of metal say another.

There is no such color as green, no such color as blue. We see a specific green, a specific blue.

Subvert yourself. Empty yourself of previous conceptions. It wouldn't be a very interesting journey for the artist if he or she already knew the destination. The artist teams up with chance. Chance always joins in. The artist makes a point of using every fluke or aberration that happens to pop up. Keys, a splotch of black ink, granulations on the surface, parquet, obstetrical instruments, butterfly wings.

Always be willing to go to extremes. If something vital must be coaxed into existence with spears and spaghetti use spears and spaghetti.

Plot nothing, plan nothing that requires calipers and permission. Charm is for jewelry, metal for madness. The currents and impulses that range through the artist's being are his or her truest guide. There must be rebellion in the act of creation. Hazy yearnings, intoxication and madness. All the flukes peculiar to the material should be allowed to come into play. There is no art without intoxication. No way is more clear than that of impulse. Treasure accidents caused by chance. Don't cut art off from the world. Every stroke, daub, and smear is a birthday. Every stimulus is an incentive for action, every drip, blob, and splatter a fertile sedition, a renaissance of rags and nails.

SALE

after Arthur Rimbaud

For sale the rusted artery of a galactic bulldozer replete with insignia, crowbar, and dreary motel curtains. A can of wax, obstinate, omnivorous, and thoroughly ecumenical. An emanation of breath glued to the sound of a thread falling through the mind of a crocodile.

For sale a fistful of birds going wild in a cloud of acoustic tinfoil. A sagebrush rattle seething with angular veins. The membrane of an area code mounted on a scarecrow. A clod of reddish-brown lighthouse dirt plucked from the eyebrow of an irrational mirror.

Mint condition memory door spangled with seaweed and twine. A fresh dream caught in the neck of a river. A pair of tennis shoes famished for careful description. A whole emotion whirled into trumpets and bulging with sound. The imponderable biology of a softball boxed in a pretty afterthought.

For sale used country. Former democratic United States. Only 230 years old. Comes with original constitution. Population not included.

For sale a 30 lbs. tattoo of pure existential thought.

For sale the fable of a nipple reflected in a spoon. A winter ballad and a song of sticks. The fervent applause of a stadium wild with the metaphysics of noise. The clarity of a haiku enshrined in water. A piece of gravity dipped in sunrise. A circle of day painted to resemble a square full of goats and zinnias. An ingot of zeros melted into romantic hardware.

For sale 400 warriors rendered in wax and a wart constructed of aphoristic drapery. A thin intestine of time rolled into thunder and counterbalanced with linoleum valentines. A vague sense of hematology excelling at reindeer. A worry thrilled with its own knitting. A suntan filtered through the sadness of a women's locker room.

For sale an agitated sock fenced with pleasantries and wolves. A moment of goo transparent as an office and awkward as a personality. For sale 300 acres of methane, five columns, three cones, and a blast of thought bandaged with ice. An antique tornado harnessed with Russian leather. Three French hens, two turtle doves, five Spanish gantries, various bullets still breathing with conflict, a stuffed trout, a regenerative lull, a dinghy full of crickets, and a partridge in a hypothetical setting of your choosing.

Hurry now. Everything must go. All is in storage and I must sell. Come and get it. Nothing is real. No truth is absolute. All it takes is courage. A willing heart, a few croissants, and a jar of interstellar gas giving birth to a $100 dollar bill.

CURRENT

Now I am going to enter on the subject of self. It is quite time I
should set myself doing something, and live no longer upon hopes.
Or ambergris or rain. Imagine entering another dimension. Use
everything you've got. Violence comes natural. Jangle the alphabet. Be
rapid and smooth. I is an island. I is nebulous. A galaxy of cells and
mitochondria. Circles, squares, valentines, docks. I is films. I is filmy.
And a bath and an ineffable river and a soft blue mineral, a blue
mineral, a cold bullfrog, squirming bullfrog, a lingering aftertaste of
bacon, a baroque garden, a tendency to listen to a distant sound, a
current for a sound, a current, a distant current, a current of sound, a
current, a sound, a current sound, a current, a distant sound.

Don't bother with length. Length is a hymn sung by teaspoon.

Use words. Words and swords. Acrobatic clouds. Push some
clouds into reality. Reality is an amalgam the window dramatizes.

The slurp of plenitude. The clank and cambric of garlic when it
thickens into gerunds. Swimming, running, eating, drinking. Meaning
noise festers in you and pink thumps against the intrigue in each
secretion of wool which is an emergence of optimism slow permea-
tions of tone imbue the personality when barley expands the wind the
body is a cantata a zipper simmers in Japanese and thickets induce a
swallow to mimic a fiddle hence the whole of it is spherical which
some perceive as vast.

Oblivion means hemorrhaging weather is a sign of tweezers.

Nature thrills with the exoticism of plums. Disease is simply
candid.

The sun will help space because when it is heated it is suffused
with something I can recognize as existential whistling and whirring a
fat flagrant sex twisted and necessary which is why it is yet palpable a
backyard garden hose consciously coiled a Saturday in Kansas a
bustling shopping mall a feeling a saddle a cumbersome daylight a
translucent yoga yoyo called yodel a crocodile on the porch a tornado
buzzing in its nerves.

Talk low, talk slow, and don't try to say too much.

Think of love or something.

It is sincere still to embody a metaphor so coconut it germinates whatever sound boldly glorifies buckskin as we feel the stinging rain there is a hurricane accurately hurled at the ground and its walls something huge something indecipherable billowing another wrinkle of cause and effect be iron be metal be goofy and yarn the world is only moving.

A minute for yellow is still an intensity a diagonal ocean those that everybody calls sugar or scarf the personality underneath one's skin blossoming in ice bountiful time a gregarious acoustic toast once bread a slice of diamond a cruet on the table a physics for understanding roads.

This is what you might call a Frasier spiral. As you can see, the curtsy is repeated again and again, until it explodes into light.

Sonnets of blue and zoo. Nuance in glue. Opacity of light pummeled by a book of saws. The saw is an important symbol. Though it might be considered pumpernickel if it is stuffed with asteroids.

A bulge while I polish a vein mouths texture the abyss yawns intervals of music it unlocks orchids of sound while devotion chugs for icicles even garlic it thickens it is on safari it is cambric and fruit I have lost the thread of what I was sewing I can hear it banging beyond the receipt because the skull widens and accommodates kilowatts of sequence those telescopes bathed in medieval birds there is a chassis for such perception called marigold. Because means are available to find something enchanting, something absorbing, something redeeming about certain irritations, since it is in onions that whatever abrades the skin in a junkyard a melody or groove with a melody in it might also awaken a concern for wood because each scratch each raft made of Bolivian logs is such a whistle till the whistle whistles insects till polemical origins of light crash into eggplant.

Biology obliges tin to intoxicate birds and ermine creates drumming about the motor from the buffet about to model the academy drapery where the sand turns into candy and the sun cudgels the ground and sails bulge and thistles thistle and hits from the jukebox dishevel the air at the machine there it is I feel the heat in a ballad of life.

Here the tar is arithmetic sudden slaps riffs rattlesnakes a lid here an engine there napkins on the saw. Amiably sudden the street maintains its mass its ease and hinge a sudden absolution coffee and cactus on a Saturday in cake over there a cellar each darkness begins a conviction a burden hence vibrato. Wispy to everyone a solo on the dock has a message of marvels terra-cotta is necessary when you are down in Memphis with a lull a pizza seeking your abdomen dough kneaded by pirates yeast caught in an eyebrow till a frontier opens the shape of the future which is husky and tan a tone of velour is once a distinction twice a sagebrush about to commit maple a plate of lasagna carried into the dining room followed by a lute a boat and a moral the data just now coming in has several forms one looks like an arm another a timid king with a crown of cherries it is all definitely a fever and can bring moans down on Thursday and merge them with canvas.

Black effluent piped through a mosaic of words that petrify flowers to brass.

There are means. Means to bring Saturday from its racket and temper it with fugues.

Diffusion begins with sight and sound, the conjuration of reindeer, lessons in life till some cruet or other appears as an intimate example of itself so fully realized it is made of many previous momentums, moments, each moment a momentum, till at last it was reasonable to assume it was not a tuba.

That's the dawn over there drooling over the edge of the paper. Rattling pieces of daylight warm the fuzz in the shrubbery. Fish flash through your kneecaps assembling the vertebrae of wisdom. Standing and distraction. The dominion of the flamingo. A gracefully religious banjo stuffing the air with huckleberry steamboat visions.

Red is a form of thinking in bulk. There is a glacier tinted with sunset, for instance, whose scale is entirely romantic, everything an embouchure of aberrant arms of ice, various thrones of rock and snow, vulgarities of cold insinuation, a saxophone in which thought is given an intensity of direction, then crushed into words as grapes into wine, a rose on the table, a glimmer of light in the window, curios on the shelves, chemistry in scabs which mimic the coffee of intimacy.

Glistens is evolve and lasagna. Age while dangerous begins sage. A proverb propeller propelling optimism as blood, or language. Or eyesight.

Steam the whole mechanical music which is an intestine as prunes or herring the sand on the road or mines where part of the darkness is bound to biology and then dissolves when a yak occurs and the wood is burning and a curb permits the sidewalk to turn silver as we eat our sushi and the magnetic walnuts pull us to salvation. The plot involves an alphabet yet wig and crow a lagoon of language if we can permit such a metaphor to thrill us because we are mostly somewhat rattled already by a saga of refraction and the furniture is so lyrical it sleeps in cumbersome movies it would seem much too defiant to introduce an inflammation to an energy so raw in its guns and consciousness it dislocates the sauté and fills the head with luster since it is either neon or miasma.

A blister button vivifies life although it is never quite as gorgeous as the day is kneaded into piccolos to mirror some plaza where those massed buzzes body forth sentences for whomever chooses to mouth them edging closer and closer to the wall. There is much open to be a hit among puddles wispy about the tar. But all this gets evaporated into clouds, and thought, which is a form of cloud, because it drifts, and has little substance, other than the occasional thunder, the occasional lightning, striking the ground, and lighting up the night, so that everything appears to be a gantry of some sort, machinery in expectation of cargo to be taken up and taken to other lands, other ports.

A satellite everybody treasures for its challenge must accurately lodge the resistance of metal refraction being a form of pain then pleasure because of the way the perceptions bend when the light passes through the water where the leaves drop everything the sun has bearded in Chinese. You might consider scratching your chin while another stadium conjurer threads the doorknob oyster with an iridescent dimple. ➤

There is a kind of proverb snatched from thought that manipulates words like diamonds. A bicycle on the blacktop blatant as a valentine.

A sheet of paper burdened with words.

A metaphor floating a sentence.

A sentence squeezed for its crucial woodwinds that feeling that churns with European laurel. A lantern the indigo prescribes by its presence as laundry. Are these just words or such meaningful fragments of orange they bracket intricate candles? Is life a cruise a ship maneuvered into a gigantic prune or a stream of consciousness pale with ecstasy? Why is a disease pushed into acoustic culture when so much water has been fenced abbreviated crashed?

Because it is bold to board a bloodmobile and evaporate. Knowledge is eggs. An egg is only a hen's way to make another egg. But there's a lot to be said for that. Think of an egg with drapery and furniture in it and you have imagined the surf of devotion cresting on the shore of appeasement. Consciousness sewn into a cricket's bikini. An ego thrilled by hints of lips I bring the fork up it glimmers there is adhesion because we are proud so proud to be actual a chemistry of gerunds.

Words are instruments a biology snatched out of the air stills from a movie puddles of sound while the tongue is a backpack muscle refractions even combs a ballad of lanterns a circumstance of nuts that's correct an archaeology a brocade hamburger and yogurt are not the same as electricity glimmers at a buckle and a buckle is not elastic not like a scarf more like wood which must be heated or moistened to bend so orange it winks so pink it boils so black and brown it balloons into hickory. A lake a bowl of cereal a grocery receipt justice is an incision this means diameter is a rug and a rebel holds a jackknife each and everything is either a means to many maps or a cackle heard in a lush century of painting never before glazed with Sunday but always opening to possibilities of sable.

An entrenched radius such as a hot dog or face-lift could do no more because chaos sticks to dreaming exploding snapping shouting dangling dappling and impasto calamities of paint Kandinsky and Pollock metabolize like candy knelling the shape of a new temper a bloodmobile at dawn those luminescences we call words a cosmos in a barrel of rainwater an insinuation of light at the top of a hill a gourmet of unleashed amaryllis a long aura of crustacean clouds fire carried by bumblebee a honey so thick and delicious it hastens infusions of French because French is busy to bursting from snow from bugs from flannel and bleachers from elephants and symmetry a pudding or irrational red.

If green ever occurred to my shirt my shirt would take it to the maximum shade and my belt would distinguish itself by astronomical accumulations I rarely wear a kimono but if I had to grapple with such a garment you can believe that barge just beyond the horizon has most of its gauze wrapped in acanthus as if cinnamon accelerated the disfigurement of writing and even became a little unsavory at times vocal to be sure fizzing out of the throat in evanescent libraries of pituitary nimbleness and if there were a king hanging about the train station at about 10:00 in the morning you could be sure something fierce and uncontrollable were going to happen that day something ghostly like remembrance or porcelain like shape.

A neck is thoughtful in sleep burlap or inlay what irritant so quickens perception that a word fulfills its mission later in the day with the coagulant viscosity of an idea supplied with blood and bravado a pucker in de Kooning a heavy cricket a cudgel of brown or green a lull between the shoulders so that a knee of no small dimension might then kneel into eternity. A dose of garage is mostly confusion. This is because the lobster has yet to be stuffed. And sincerity suckles birch. A blade and a blemish and a friendly goo wants neon. This makes everything sag. Or nail itself to an embryo of light.

A tube is soft about the vowel as everything jumps into consciousness finding means to exist as knocks or columns crust bulges various speeds of stampede burdened with the latitude of muscle and bone possible to an understanding of unstoppable energies which is precisely why a tablet of paper is sometimes lined and sometimes longer than normal or salad dressing eludes description or pork chops are a surgical disgrace but an important song of meat blending biography with bone. A moth is not a mouth but put a you in the moth and the moth becomes a mouth. A large powdery insect eating time and lacing space with the flutter of gospel.

Space is so shape has somewhere to form a weight. Mass. Density. Convertible or sandwich. A statement like a saddle. Creaking leather. Stirrups. Embossing. Beatitude.

Button is mostly pearl while a barrel full of nuts flirts with mirth and Paris is how a membrane in a bog might function as a sail like the pronoun I which is recommended for water because water here obtains a busy function an inundation or cloud preparing to condense and fall and become a river puddles drips drops spit salt salsa. Splitter splatter melon maelstrom of aesthetic pluck plunged in insurrection.

There is blood radiant only in some affirmation because a monstrous snake winks like a flagstone. This means the asterisk will not become a doctrine but simulate the sheen of candy which the bouillon bugles as a certain cement selected for its integrity and ability to dry quickly gains roughness by use and encroachment.

Nor sun like I horse gantry bound how devout melt yak grotesque abstraction road lurch. It is safe to say grapple.

It often happens about a button that a grotesque fuzz burdens the bug with a big idea of Paris or a rough horse motel whose proximity to thirst enlarges you because oak argues pine on a sail of agitated canvas most people here would agree that the miniskirt is making a comeback and blood and sage and isn't machinery something the way it mumbles till you see a bird in the mirror.

Never absorb an eyeball then cage it in cotton or the burning chrome of a city in summer electricity drives these pages the fingerboard of a fork a sawhorse a vibrant diagonal everything in conflict is ever a meteorology it drips refraction about a buckle it often happens that many Arizona corrals suggest the metabolism of an oyster might be uninterrupted by Spanish while a suite of goofy absolutions attach the voice to a zigzag with an area code light as pop. Because can can can pumpernickel an ode means a helium mostly scarf can dive that bumblebee and knell lettuce there is a nail tossed in the shrubbery which drums itself fat. Gout now the crustacean bruise a salad figured on such a neck the mines' occurrence did a kimono to nervous the gun because emotion is necessary to lunge at a lush cordovan which we were instructed to letter.

Never wear a kimono in a coal mine.

Tube bundled in Cytherea many crusts invite meringue because laughing is everybody's gerund why is the mouth opening beyond the intestine there is a whole skeleton dancing a silver pain and an acetylene lilac and a crumbling delicacy since a lama whiffs thunder a critical spine embodies corduroy only flannel shoulders the generality of flight transformation is a miracle sometimes it has been stone or bone housed in buffalo a bolt on a door whence a Montana shack a butte and a dot and a cloud with a lavender vertebrae.

Favor the cereal with cinnamon while lugging a bank road use more history fungus is convolution equity is mood a mayonnaise swan here the essence is cumulative mostly rapids and rapture not a matter of hydrogen so much as cellophane it seals well and a feather rumbles with sideburns here is an occasion to inspect a creamery is that a stratosphere or a string of words infested with herring as a sauna renders us glistening a kimono blossoms on a doorknob and somewhere beyond doubt and acceptance a bubble pops and suddenly the world is both for and against the fantasia of borders spangling scaffolds and time zones and shudders of tender gaffe.

The C Major of this life turns slippery on the pages. A gleam from a realm of night inheres in the lacquer of a terrible staircase called digestion. The burden of the incommunicable. The iron of wrath. The lungs of the yak forging Mongolian steam.

Plant yoga in a catalogue even a backbone opines its ardor then Saturday climbs the street as one declaration after another stirs for the arena which is virtually a dream beyond the pliers rigid there like a gabardine knapsack indigo beyond an acute derby of golf or a flashlight critical of the whole palpable thumb. An orchid I heat with a smack of unbridled perception offers an appeasement a cackling crackling sun of overwhelming denim nibbles gravity into a seesaw creating an aroma of sand and supposition a crisp sense of hypothesis personal as diffusion the perfect warmth of a fable whose bubbles rebuke the world.

There Was A Time

There was a time when people rode in carriages affirming the joy of being with accordions and lungs. If a meteor seared through the sky and hit the ground with explosive force, they would stop to get out and look at it. If it was of moderate size and radiated glad tidings of extraterrestrial propinquity, they would keep it. If it did not they would toss it aside where it would lie forgotten among weeds, rusty ploughshares, and bits of obsidian. If a small child were found inside, they would raise him until he became a man of infinite capability, and wore a red cape, and blue tights.

There was a time when birch and aspen flickered on the hillsides and leaves of copper and bronze were blown across the landscape which was popularly considered to be a long irregular sentence spoken by an old man.

It was a time of innocence and bloomers. It was a time of caverns and dots. Mountains sulked. Meadows vacillated between goldenrod and amaryllis. Everything seemed silly, yet sad, like the twang and whine of a country guitar. Magpies on barbed wire mocked the ricketiness of existence while swallows laced alphabets of dusk and exultation.

The sky was bold and blue. Clouds pitched through the air like galleons. Consciousness floated the flotsam of thought. Pessimism trembled with optimism. Optimism cried for cubism. Occasionally a mass of vitrified bricks fused together to form a paragraph with five pairs of legs and intaglio engraving on its abdomen. This was then slapped until it pitched forward shaping declensions with its spools and creating a habitat for thought and glamorous improbabilities.

It was a time of far horizons and inflammations of sound. Cantatas in cans. Loons in bassoons. The garrulity of a horse's muzzle. Fruit and tools and gargoyles dribbling semantic bremsstrahlung. Everyone dressed in silk and denim. Buttons were made of ebony and pearl and the DNA of winter. Distance was considered a genuine tissue of time and worn like a hat. Velocity was busy with the colors of hypothesis and endless transformative conflict. Vibrations of all sorts were zipped into words and accentuated with sunspots. Teleological centipedes. Ontological hinges. What exists. What is. What am I. It was that kind of world, that kind of time. Whirls of dust and air pouring out of the sky. Misty placentas oozing lyceums of breeze and drizzle.

Everything had a story. Everything had a soul. Floors creaked in old hotels. There was gladness and glass in all the windows. The violence of poetry was actual and steel. Salaries were salt. Jobs were pepper. Highways were long and led you deep into the glitter of night.

This was a time beyond time. It was the time of nothingness and string. Sonnets bleeding diamonds and myriad bits of light.

BETTER HOMES AND ABSTRACTIONS

My wife and I want to move but we cannot agree on the sort of place we'd like to inhabit. I want to live in a laboratory for testing ottomans. She wants to live in a jukebox full of long corridors and stratospheric counterpoints. I want to live in a limestone cantata in Anchorage, Alaska. She wants to live in a blade of grass with thirty-two rooms and a washcloth made of moonlight. I want to live in a climate of words whose clumsiness is supple as a minuet. She wants to live in a logarithm carpeted with magnolia petals. She insists that her logarithm be constructed of the finest irrational numbers available and that all the windows are orthogonal polynomials and all the doors are alluring solutions to space and time. Our realtor is frustrated, but stimulated by our many requirements. She shows us house after house after house. Each time we stomp on the floor to check for grammar and syntax. The house of language is not a box with a roof on it but a mansion of many appliances. Syllables, sensations, plumbing. "I want to live in a texture," my wife insists. "What kind of texture," I ask. "Any texture," she replies. "All textures." I assure her that the house of language is a text of infinite texture. But my wife is more mathematically inclined than I. She worries about the geometry. "What about shape," she asks. "What about depth and volume? What about length and width? What about fortitude and shirts?" The house of language has all these things. The house of language is built of thought, which is a lumber like pine, with knots and resin. Which is a species of reason. Which is an adventure of corners and knobs. Which is a suite of assertions. Which is a tabernacle of words. Which is a protective shell. Which is a tegument or rind. Which is a melon. Which is a thing put forward on a vine. Which is a ramification. Which is an eidolon, a fruit that ripens in the mind. "But the mind must have a head," asserts my wife, "and a skull to keep it dry." And this is true. But not so true it pleads concrete. Or the testament of form. It is more like a dirigible, or balloon. Something that rises, then drifts through the sky.

SQUIRT

My brain sometimes has a tendency to squirt thoughts. Big thoughts little thoughts. Brown thoughts gray thoughts. Red thoughts blue thoughts. Hot thoughts cold thoughts. Thoughts about feathers and pearls and Nickelodeons. Thoughts about velvet and veneration thoughts about tools thoughts about fools thoughts about Americans and cages and daydreams. Thoughts about utopia thoughts about balloons. Thoughts about rocks thoughts about thoughts. Thoughts that drift thoughts that enslave thoughts that entice fat thoughts thin thoughts wry thoughts thoughts that bloom in emulsion. What is a thought? A thought is a sunbeam crushed into film. A movie in the mind. A broken headlight and a jack in the road. Raw meat. Raw art. Raw hide. Light held together by string. Canteen smeared with blood. A nose adhering to an elusive scent. An elusive scent. An occupying energy in the form of a chair. Tag on a shirt. An incandescent jet. Jam in a jar red transparent and sweet. How is a thought different from an idea? An idea has escalation and steps and moves up and down and a thought just floats. An idea might be drawn or written down and a thought might also be drawn or written down but an idea is diagonal and neon and a thought is reckless and pasty. Clouds in the head. Presentiment. Premonition. Pea. A shovel in advance of a broken arm.

YOGURT

Thirty years ago I was living in a hotel in Arcata, California and my diet consisted chiefly of yogurt and brown rice. I was a student, attending Humboldt State, and my hotel room was small but comfortable. I was immersed in romantic and metaphysical poetry, and gorged myself on Blake and Shelley, Traherne and Donne. I cooked the rice on a hotplate, and rinsed my dishes in a small porcelain sink which was recessed into a small narrow niche in the wall. My one window overlooked a roof in the center of the building, surrounded by walls on all sides so as to form a hollow of vents and rippled tar. A painting of a gypsy wagon, by Vincent Van Gogh, kept me company on the wall by my bed, and a small wooden desk abutted the pale yellow wall where I sat with my back to the window, poring over sentences like "The world is unknown, till the value and glory of it be seen: till the beauty and the serviceableness of its parts is considered."

I purchased my rice and yogurt from a small grocery store on the other side of a square in which a statue of President McKinley faced west, austere and dignified. I luxuriated in the modesty of my circumstances, and the flavor and texture of the yogurt which I lifted in my spoon from its paper container, echoed and reaffirmed the sparkle of my sumptuous austerity.

Yogurt is an enigma. It invites and defies description. It is like magnetism. It exerts a force I cannot see or identify. It is neither an elegant food, like *charlotte russe,* nor exciting and raw, like sushi. It is a tenuous, indistinct flavor, much like the wisp of melody emerging in the bass of Schubert's *Impromptu in A-flat.* There is just enough flavor, just enough suggestion of blueberry or cherry, to let you know you're eating something meant to be eaten, and not wool filler or spackling compound. It is the flavor of implication, the auspicious prompting of cream rather than the stern proposals of steak or disquieting manifestos of beets, the flavor of innovation rather than the weary protocol of cheese or Weltschmerz of veal. It is not a sumptuous Titanic luring the appetite with ominous slabs of bacon and butter but a Spartan portion of cream intended to be consumed modestly with a view toward the fragility of life and the eternal curdling of the stars.

My eating habits changed after I left Arcata. I began treating myself to rich and copious pastas, zingy fajitas and wickedly goopy *sacher tortes*. Yogurt became a remote dream. I became sluggish and fat. Finally, out of desperation, I returned to yogurt as a spurned lover turns to the solitude and rigors of mountain climbing to purge the heart of its heavy gloom.

Art is a refuge for mimetic comportment, observed Adorno. In art the subject exposes itself, at various levels of autonomy, to its other, separated from it and yet not altogether separated. This is yogurt all over. This is yogurt through and through. Mixing yogurt with words is like a blend of the rational with the irrational, the palpable and clear with the chimerical and obscure. The mouth fills with creamy aporia, a dollop of alimentary ambiguity. One wonders if this is food one is ingesting, or music. If music be the food of love, then yogurt is an E flat unrolled *Allegro di molto* out of a bright chromatic spoon.

It is imperative the yogurt is unstirred, and that the fruit is on the bottom. I do not enjoy the preemptive indeterminacy of pre-stirred yogurt. I prefer the charm of a deferred pleasure, a chaste, undisturbed curdle postponing a zesty scherzo. The voluptuous lyricism of an Alsatian *kugelhopf* or the polytonal fantasia of a *chaud-froid* of chicken in jelly are fine, but what I really enjoy are spoonfuls of yogurt slowly and methodically maneuvered into my mouth until the fruit—a gleaming layer of raspberries or strawberries or bananas or cherries—reveals its virginal hue and beckons the pitch of my palate with the timbre of its flute.

NEW GRIND

I need a new grind of coffee a thick black brew tasting of electrons and birds. A coffee so thick it clanks and clatters like tools tossed into the back of a truck.

A grind so alive it shudders with stupefaction.

A grind so emphatic it quivers with baptism and blues.

I propose a new grind a brew of propane and propulsion a blend complex as an insurance claim a commotion a confluence a tumult of flavor swirls and curls of unbridled aroma a grind like a U-haul practical and temporary a brew like a junkyard informal as mud yet estimable as lianas and orchids in Brazilian rain.

A grind pertinent as black pepper in a yellow cupboard uncompromising as garlic shrill as a phalanx of flutes transcendent as a photograph of heaven candid as a cauliflower exotic as Pittsburgh.

A grind fresh and quick as a border collie primordial as a crustacean intractable as asphalt smooth as Burlington rails eventual as rust implacable as death balletic as life and palpable as both.

Something philosophical. Something zingy and metaphysical. Something like Spinoza spinning a web of lightning in the highlands of Peru.

Not a coffee so much as a way of life, a song and a concertina on a Parisian street a volcano erupting on a south Pacific island Jimi Hendrix setting a guitar on fire a dimension a remedy a boiler-room an indefinite article a flock of cranes a riot at the zoo.

A fulcrum. A Belgium. A basso profundo. An ineffable brew.

Transient Notion

Computers and airplanes have made our city wealthy and it is full of coffee houses. Everywhere you look are latte stands and coffee houses. You'd think the city was built on caffeine. Caffeine and software.

This afternoon I have chosen to go to a coffeehouse called The U Turn. The door is open allowing the flow of brisk October breezes to freshen the interior of the coffeehouse and give easy access to the customers sitting at one of the sidewalk tables.

The air outside is bright and moist and imbued with haze. The atmosphere inside is enlivened by the hubbub of voices, the exertions and bam! bam! bam! of the barista pounding her espresso filter, a portly young woman with long black hair done up in a knot, a tuft of hair at the top of her head. She is wearing a tight-fitting blue blouse with a low neckline revealing an ample cleavage and skin a little lighter in tone than a latte. "What would you like?" she asks me. "A single mocha," I reply, "a single short mocha, if there is such a thing." "You can have anything you want," she robustly replies, "within the coffee world, that is."

I sit down. A copper elephant sits on its haunches at the base of a lamp reading a newspaper. The fringe of the lampshade is purple and consists of pieces of braided string. I reach for André Breton's *Anthologie de l'humour noir* and notice an overhead fan twirling in my spoon.

The coffee house is crowded. Voices mingle and clash. Behind me, an Asian woman in a jogging suit is telling her friend about a coyote that was chased into a downtown elevator by a flock of angry crows. Her voice is cheerful and soft and pleasant to hear. I go on reading a fragment by Xavier Forneret. Promises and truth are like balls that people toss each other back and forth and that remain hanging in the air. My attention, engorged by the aforementioned balls, is momentarily detoured by three middle-aged women animatedly talking at the table next to me. The heaviest of the three, a woman with short blonde curly hair, is giving a vigorous account of her children and domestic tribulations. Her kids want a pet, a dog or a cat. She jokes about getting goldfish. Or a transient, ha ha ha ha.

I imagine this woman and her family with a transient for a pet. I picture a gaunt man in his early sixties who resembles Samuel Beckett. A large aquiline nose and deep sunken eyes, furrowed brow and prominent cheekbones. A face full of crags and gnarly despondency. I imagine him sitting in an armchair, reading Hegel or Proust, happy at last to have a place in the world.

Or would they keep him in the garage, supplying him with bowls of food and water in exchange for displays of affection? Would they expect him to do tricks? Fetch sticks? Coax him to put his head in their laps? Take him for walks in the park? Clean up with a plastic baggie after evacuating his bilious bowels?

An absurd proposal, yes. The notion was nothing more than an inane attempt at humor. I think the woman actually felt embarrassed after saying it. A sense of having gone too far. Though by then it was too late. Some things are ineluctable. Some things reek of destiny. Some things spill into this life large and axiomatic from the tongue of Fate. If there is such a thing as Fate. Perhaps there is only desire. But desire is plenty, let me tell you.

All it takes is an impulse. A simple impulse. The rest is momentum. Once the impulse gets the proverbial ball rolling momentum takes over. If no external force acts on a body in motion there is no change in momentum. There was no change in momentum. I arrived compliant and doting on hands and knees when I delivered my little surprise, the fingers of the woman's left hand dangling idly and bare to the frolic of my moist and actual tongue.

A BRAIN

Here then is a brain, an organ, a globe of juice and artifact, a globe
full of life and convolution, crisp thoughts of oboes, soliloquies and
solidarity, passions theorized into seasons and dyes, bits and scraps of
denim, ideas big as Scandinavia. A big brain, a happy brain, a drama-
tic brain in bubbles, in a big glass drum, on view as on television,
you've seen it before, a brain immersed in science fiction, a late night
movie, here it is again, an emblem of thought, an emblem of think-
ing, thinking and thought minus a body, minus instincts and needs,
minus awkwardness and mobility, minus caulking gun and paycheck,
beard, face, and razor, tongue and cheek and lariat and leek. A fore-
taste of eternity, of a phantom existence, the life of a ghost, a life of
subtlety and nuance, shades and pastels, memories and pools, dark
secret pools of reflection, the kind of pools we find in caves, in sub-
terranean recesses, pools fed by underground streams, moisture
bleeding down mineralized walls, trickles of silver water feeding a
pool of blind white fish. The kind of world Samuel Beckett might
envision, an Irish fellow growing wrinkled and sage in Paris, a city full
of dynamism and open markets, bins full of pears and apples, egg-
plant and squash, fresh new ideas, galvanizing provocations, the sort
of thing admired in Paris, the sort of thing that will get you beat up in
Dublin. City, hamlet, brain. A brain full of figures, a naked brain, a
brain on view, a brain on exhibit, a brain in a bubbling glass cylinder,
a brain with electrodes attached, and a mechanical voice, and a mech-
anical ear, a brain capable of response, a brain in a bubbling glass
cylinder like an octopus in an aquarium, a rich reflective existence
finally freed, finally liberated from the aches and pains of the body,
the trappings and musculature of the body and its fragile condition,
its tendency to slip, its tendency to fall, its overpowering need to eat,
to seek shelter, to contribute parts of itself to another body, a slightly
different body, a body with a slightly different set of needs, never a
completely perfect match, no, but lots of stimulation, a body like all
other bodies craving attention, craving caresses, craving flight and
freedom, freedom to do what it wants, freedom to float, freedom to

sit down, freedom to make words, words of all sorts, bronze words for monumental thoughts, paper words for meteors and snow. A body with a tongue, a spine, a pair of arms, a pair of legs, a scrotum like a paragraph full of fluid and seed, a pair of breasts and a system for reproduction, for growing another body, another body inside this body, another body like a fruit, a fruit on the branch, a scion, an elaboration, an ambassador to the future, an ambassador carrying memories of one body to the ears and nostrils of another body, another body with another brain, a wing nut and an epic direction, a fresh divertimento, thought and reflection wiggling in a sea of salt and light.

MARSDEN HARTLEY'S GLOVES

let's pan for gold, blow off steam, rub
a glass rod with silk
& make electricity

dance on the head of a pin. Prose is all cartilage
poetry a fin. Like as the waves
make toward the pebbled shore, so do our minutes
hasten to their end, each changing place

with that which goes before. The old myth
of artistic purity has many active volcanoes
constantly boiling into discourse. There is a touch
of cruelty in wax, & a poem requires a meaning
that has to be dealt with on its own terms, like a paperweight

enclosing a suspension bridge, or the big orange drum
of a cement truck going round
& round. The robustness of candor, the abraded vigor

of Marsden Hartley's gloves
& garden shears, all those tough, vivacious browns
inventing an emotion, a way to be in the world
like Mary Tyler Moore. A metaphor is made of shadows

like anyone else, even Sardinia
rendered in color several centimeters thick. Beauty
requires a large subjective framework
incidental as a grocery receipt

revealing a pair of breasts in a lacy black bra
To be a fool
is to bend time
& space

while enjoying breakfast in a sumptuous robe
of probability

Try picturing a cat
attached to Egypt
Cultures intermingle
& the mouth is a laboratory for testing words, a pair of dice

tossed on the dark
mahogany of a Montana bar. There is the music of the toolbox
& the music of the loin. The music of the mundane
& musk ox & salt. But a glove, a true glove

should fit the hand like the dark
in a radio, like the glitter
of stars bleeding through the turquoise of a Mediterranean dusk
Nothing beats a good pair of gloves, & a pair of worn brown chafed
gloves is a glossary of new & familiar sensations, a blend of the
    known
& the unknown. The slide of content into the fingers of form
& the expansion of form by the wriggle of foraging fingers.

Color Noctambule

At night the colors crawl down off the wall with their shrill contours smeared with excitement and tell us of goldfinches and jujubes. They jabber of controversies of brick and swimming pools monastic as soup. They tell us we are blind and that they are nervous and teetering on rain. We say nothing because we are asleep. We are asleep and do not listen. Green walks around in a dark pine forest and blue says we have a friend in osmosis. A red rose gathers the lips of representation and makes a bouquet of syntax and breath. A yellow sun walks across the sky in a black robe fringed with golden beads. A pink blob imagines it is a pig and then explodes into bacon. A gray mist envelops a hill and a tattered cloud vomits a mountain. Brown mimics the sound of heavy machinery digging the earth. A black elastic belt with a thin white stripe emerges from a theory of light reeking of desire and gun smoke. The alarm goes off and the colors shatter into metal. Daylight bursts golden over the mountains. Everything becomes inexplicable as space; a knife on the counter, a thought in the throat.

CROCUS

Worry is red. Alert and surgical. But what does it mean to be pink? Go down the escalator with big wet songs. Ride a gallant horse into the light of a hemorrhaging sun. Somewhere vague and heathery, like the downs of England. You will find that pink means knuckle. Particle physics and bugs.

Today I feel like exploding out of my skin to conjecture a life in green. Although red is a strange way to express that.

Those blades of grass are reciting Whitman. They smell of roses and myrrh. Either sing or sit down. Cambric and silk have been embroidered into letters, each about to fall from one perception to another. Because green is full of life. And there is a lid on my head. And zinnias and zithers and zephyrs and zippers. And the lid opens and out comes a flock of goldfinch. Membranous folds. Perpetual laryngeal headlights. A past participle agape on a legal pad.

Thought is muscular, vellum and toil. The soft thin churn of revelation.

A song is a bunch of melody crammed with words. Dye mingled with cotton. Notice my shirt. Each button is a world inscribed in ivory. They move and talk and gargle auguries of rags. Not because they are aglow and sporadic but because they are birds.

Some things are never the same. And some things, like radius and pi and circumference, are infested with proposition.

Here I am opening the door to another dimension. There is licorice on your lip and a sentence struggling to get out, a state of being, an élan reckless as a tongue. Lips moving together to produce a chain, a sequence, a rapture, because ivory is opaque and beautiful and pummeled by harpsichord. Because DNA burlesques the foible of life and yet it continues to resist the society of hyphens. Because there is a pair of eyes searching for detail. Because there are clouds dropping bits of heaven. Because heaven is a dime enshrined in your wrist.

This is a piece of air, still as the water in a well.

Imagine a paragraph in which each word is deliriously alive, leaping into the shrubbery of language, all that semantic lumber hammered to the lapel of the sky, the big open sky, which is made of ink and paper. Imponderable acts of turquoise. Coral and coal and caramel and catfish.

Most eyes tend to be placed in the head just above the nose, which is round and wonderful, like a hill, or a Kashmir goat.

What is death? A dialogue with a man sitting on a dock. Frankenstein cold and shivering and full of ethereal humors, cirrus, whatever breath fills with these things.

Noses are dizzyingly multifarious.

Say something. Anything. Infect the air with insurgent ideas.

There are many ways to die into sense. Gleams, glooms, heat, beets, mops, and immoderate expectations. Squirrels and towering chestnut trees, a pretty red mug in which coffee steams. Refrigerated mist. A movie is just a movie until it explodes in scintillating sensations. Lather it, splash it, shave it. The lightning in my mouth pulses spurts ejaculates. And yet, I don't know what precisely to say.

When you think of struggle, what comes to mind? The sonnets of Ted Berrigan? The logic of crosswalks? See that bucket? It is full of minnows.

In any case, an eyeball will always be an eyeball. It doubles, sometimes, as architecture.

Can a word pulse? You bet it can. But what controls the color changes? The ultimate controlling force is the central nervous system. By lengthening the modulus of stimulation we can enrich the stimulus of meanings and so create a yak whose day begins by cleavage. As above, so below. The white pieces indicate snow. The red pieces urge welding and coal.

Sensation leads to reflection. This is not a prose poem it is an ice cube tinkling in a glass of chilled chimeras, a flavor in the mind weighed carefully at the assay office. Delirious nonsense. The metaphysics of shoes. All to say the sun is bright. Once we start admitting abstract objects, there is no end. Because glass is an event not an object. Just as the theory of electrons would be none the worse for having first occurred to its originator in the course of some absurd dream.

Duck decoys circling a birdbath. Blossoms heaped in the gutter.

I like to run. This is one reason to not trust optimism. Another is to melt into someone's life, its bulk and mass and density and sassafras.

Cork in a bottle.

There is an emotion in me that is hard to express. The world is round and crammed with detail. Why is nonsense nonsense? It is a form of running. Though there is something lacking to this logic. What is needed is a gear for pulling a heavy idea, a large open way of handling words.

Are those eyes or big fat diamonds? Everybody says it is music, lapels and people talking in formal postures. Raw and powerful nonsense, a crocus of bricks. Still, the movies go on bewitching us with stories, feathers and wings ever open to the idea of fluidity. A minor key dripping with gauze.

Suddenly the huge rock moved. Whom does this concern? Are you religious? Blatant? Biodegradable?

Much sense makes perfect nonsense. Go ahead. Abuse the sun. Knock three times. The ontology of abstract objects is part of the sunlight too. We are not in a position to jettison any of part it, except as we have substitute devices ready to hand that will serve the same essential purposes. Tattoos deep as evening. Dashboards to mimic the geometry of grapes. Dots in a cartoon. Divinity in thunder.

Hand me that idea. There is a cell phone vibrating and ringing on the table. Which is a miracle of technology. Like thistles in the meadow. Let us only be a little more discreet about life in the suburbs.

Grass is an expression of shawls.

There is a window in which reality assumes the form of shrubbery, all of it smoldering with sudden daylight.

The sounds in a stream of speech are mostly rocks. Tornados and saddles and galloping horses. Everything out west is warm and leather. Old man with a heart of gold. Begin to pop out of yourself. The west is lousy with metal. Buffets with deviled eggs. Shops just beginning to open. Death is an adventure, thin ice with intricate patterns. Life is derived from the interior. Bronze lion dribbling water into a stone fountain.

Let us keep our diaries while the day is colliding with dreams and the sun is bouncing down the street. Meaning ham and cheese. Veins on a hand. Wildcat lapping water. Milk and butter in a lonely motel.

Paragraph crammed with thought. Dip it in Shakespeare while the sun lingers on the horizon.

My left toe is black. Some call it Nike toe. Water rippling in a Pendleton pond. Waterfall in my wallet lacquered and black. Pastel eyeball.

Sight leads to thought, red and green like Christmas, boardwalk full of tourists.

Set of longhorns mounted on the hood of a red El Dorado.

Gravestones capped in snow.

Here is my I.D. Clumps of ice on the surface of Titan.

What is pain? Pain is icicles. Pain is olives. Pain is anything on the obverse side of pleasure. This is so hard to get across. Like clay molded into women while dreams of maypop flow through the mind.

Worry is wherever emotion is sweat. It is natural to worry. There are many things to worry about. The nonexistence of isolated free quarks, wonky lighthouses, and the laws of foreign cities. Enemies. *Trompe-l'oeil* textures. Virtue in rags. Torchlight processions. An octopus crawling through a bonfire. The etymology of zero. The explosion of a hydrogen bomb. A radical, exact and invincible loyalty to certain insights into the relation between artistic and nonartistic experience.

Dinosaurs, snow globes, hatchets with rubber blades. Paul Revere's garden in the north of Boston. All those little dimples on the skin of an orange.

Clingstone. An earring on the laundry room floor.

MIRÓ'S BLUES

Blue 1. Palma de Mallorca, March 4, 1961

Nothing sags. Everything floats. The entire canvas is a deep, alluring blue. A dream of blue, an enchantment in blue.

It is a tyranny of sugar. A sweet dictatorship of blue. What is illusion and what is reality are arbitrary equations. If there is sunburn there are also atoms. So that blue is a circumstance of air. So that balconies are cumulative and coal is quicker than understanding butter. So that words are full of trembling sounds. So that meaning is a value, a color, a nectar for the eyes. So that it becomes necessary to float a utopia.

This blue is intense. It is larger than summer. It rips you out of your bones and pulls you into the painting. It has the savor of a dimension detached from this world. But why how detached from this world when it is also so emphatically immediate, so irrefutably present?

A thought is made of nerves.

A blue overflowing with crisis and resolution.

It would seem an easy task to liberate the spirit. It is, after all, a spirit. What walls can stop that which has no material substance? But it is not easy to liberate the spirit. There are immaterial walls more powerful than actual walls. Walls of dogma. Walls of belief. The epoxy of opinion. The dead thud of thought killed by an anemic curiosity.

An image becomes emotion when it comes in through the eyes and abandons itself to the cellos of rumination. To a rhapsody on the serenity of blue. There is nothing so intermingled it cannot be carried out of the throat in a song of seeds. An acre of meaning ploughed in leisure might be nourished by interrelation. Seeing is seeing. Seeing is breezy and energetic. Seeing is juncture and oak. Seeing is brick. Seeing is a sculpture made of beef. Seeing is a cow made of pearls. Seeing lets us out of ourselves if we are so willing to pulse with meaning. This can be a mood.

A good place to begin seething with color is to smell what there is to smell in temperature and compote. To begin a catechism of waterfalls and living prodigies of fact salient with bone.

What is real and what is not real. What is illusion and what is reality. If something gives you a strong sensation there is a good possibility that that thing is true. But sometimes such a sensation comes from things that are elsewhere. There are realities beneath the surface. There are realities that resist the twist of authority. Reality isn't routine. Reality is savage. Reality is elsewhere. Existence is elsewhere. It is the taste of a cashew. It is the shape of a grease stain on the floor of a garage. It is the pop and crackle of a fire in a stone hearth walking the walls between the notes of a nervous sonata. It is the heart teeming with feeling. It is a sky invented by hyacinths. It is famous as an alphabet kissing a piece of air. It is the sound of a membrane accelerating a handstand. It is imprisoned in nothing but its own majestic grammar. It is sewn together with bells and huckleberry. It is worn with locomotion. It is buttoned with clouds.

Darkness is necessary to the light like a particle of eye and that which exists to eat sunlight. The atoms which are blue and the heat which is red and the jacket that has that scenery and the externality which is there where individuality continues painting, all this and there is hay when samples of speech churn with heterogeneity, all this and simultaneity melting behavior, all this is axiomatic and welcome in thermometers.

If existence is collision then it is obvious that thought unfolds in emotion like hydrogen. It is a ladder in Mali that will never be quite understood without hands and feet.

A quality of logic is conjured here, a fugue of luscious indeterminacy. You open your mouth to sing and no sound comes out. Nothing but the color blue.

Singing is everything. Singing is obvious and skin. An empathy. A contiguity, like glue.

The world is clay. The universe is blue.

The painting is a dream of immanence, a quiddity. It exudes an inner essence, a lumen, like the light inside a plum. It is simultaneously in this world and outside of this world. It postulates the existence of what does not exist. But what does not exist exists so insistently that it creates a sensation of extreme imponderability. An idea, a philosophy of blue.

In the middle of the canvas, just to the left of center, is a red rectangle. Surrounding it is an aura of red, a diffusion of red emanating from the rectangle as if the shape were warm and alive. It closely resembles the rod-shaped mitochondria in the cell of a living organism. It is the protein, the energy feeding the blue, making it large and contrapuntal, like a stillness splattered with flutes.

Eight black dots constellate the blue of the canvas. They seem to bleed through the blue, like spots of ink on a moistened napkin.

Why eight? Why not nine, or ten, or fourteen?

There are eight musicians in an octet and eight reasons to choose a John Deere irrigation engine. Eight white pawns and eight black pawns in a game of chess. Plato has eight spheres of different colors surrounding the luminous pillars of heaven. In the Pythagorean system eight represents solidarity and stability. There are eight important strategic acupuncture points. Eight parts of speech in Latin, as in English. In Chaldean numerology, eight is infinity, paradise regained. In Buddhist tradition eight is regeneration and rebirth. There are eight Taoist genii or immortals. Eight beatitudes. Eight ways to beat stress. Eight ways to change the world. Eight ways to beat Wal-Mart. Eight ways to hide a hearing aid. Eight ways to maximize space. Eight ways to keep your prostate healthy. Eight legs on a spider. Eight planets in our solar system.

On the eighth day of his trip out west, which is a romance postulated on distance, Arthur Rimbaud got hungry and shot a rabbit. He noted the pink of its entrails and wrote a letter to Walt Whitman. Dear Walt, it said, today I saw the color of innocence. It is pink.

Numbers are clumsy. This is why existence is onyx. An eyeball filled with August.

Knowledge is repaired by moss. Nostalgia does not mean the surface of anything is cellular and a lighter brown is perpetuated by hardwood. It means Indiana in the heat. It means the Balearic Islands are a perfect place for blue to happen.

There are laminations of meaning everywhere. A spoon or a toma-hawk can be weighed in the mind like a philosophy. This is the utopia of construction. Miró has created in oil the dialectical ether in which art takes place. It is a means to enchant the disenchanted world. It is a garden of color in an interstice of light.

Running diagonally across the canvas, from right to left, is a thin black line. It is barely perceptible. It is so thin and delicate that it assumes the power of eternity. A skeleton trumpeting death. The joy of candy. Spray from a rock. Electricity in lemons. A head full of heaven.

It is fragile and tough like a cloud tacked to a wall.

It cannot be denied. It insists on being there. It has a reason for being there. A purposeless purpose. Its own rationale. It sticks to the mind like a street. A dye. The gaze of a skull.

Go ahead laugh. If everything is mechanistic then why are predicates occasionally moist?

Energy is mass squared and painted blue. When the fire has been frozen a piece of Spanish will temper it and help it into palpability.

This is the dance of the mind on the head of a pin. It is undertaking to see what is seen. It is sensitive to the allegory of knuckles. It quadruples the sense the way a mouth opens letting out thought.

If the words are palpitating the reality is unattached and the part that is floating is a tongue and the atoms continue to affiliate with judo.

Do not underestimate the octave of a dot. It is the color of fact. The color of fact seethes with blind forces. A slight wind. Tinfoil moving across a picnic table. A cloud stripping itself of mountains.

When skin becomes dramatic it is time to ooze topaz. This is how the color blue was invented. It was a little place to have an engine react to reading. Eight black dots and a thin black line and a surface crawling with thought.

Blue II. Palma de Mallorca, March 4, 1961.

Here again blue. All blue. A dagger of red extends down to the left. To the right is a line of black dots of varying size. They have been arranged horizontally. They might be pebbles on a beach. Each dot is punctually, insistently there: a pinch of oblivion. The silence in a bell before it has rung.

The dagger of red is noticeably darker at the top, suggesting a hilt. It floats. It is not stabbing, not sticking in anything. Yet it has weight and reality. Its lines are not well delineated. The form is evident but its lines are strangely ambiguous. It has been brushed into place, not stabbed. Not thrust. It has been willed into being by bristle. Oozed from a man's hand. Flick of the wrist. Deft strokes. The form is compelling, dynamic, but lacks solidity. There has been no attempt to make it actual. Its presence has the gratuitous charm of art, the felicity of presence without the burden of intent. This knife cannot cut meat. It cannot slice. It murders its own objectivity by a blade of lambent red. It is being and nothingness. It is pertinence without purpose. It is pointedly superfluous, shape as an end in itself. It is so cut from intent that it impacts the eyes as a pure penetration. It is a provocation of color. It draws the attention left while the black dots draw the attention to the right. The dots create a strong illusion of directed impulse. They appear to be moving to the right with some secret intent. Their progress appears, even, to be tilting the tip of the red knife to the left. It is a counterpoint not simply of shape and color but of that which appears to have purpose and that which does not.

There are thirteen dots (the largest being number five, counting from the left) but this is completely arbitrary. More appear to be coming from the other side. What elicits this illusion is the last, thirteenth dot: it resides at the very edge of the canvas, as if it had just popped into view.

There is a narrative at work here, an allegory, a proverb, a pointed message in the guise of a red dagger and thirteen dots. But how can we begin to unravel the meaning of this riddle before we know what the riddle is? And if this painting is hugged in color like skin wrapped around bone, a jubilant value of keen, unmitigated sensation, why drag allegory into the picture?

Perhaps I do not understand allegory. In a world where signs are common as flannel, in a world where symbols bubble with books, how can there not be allegories? A better piece of light is juggled when there has been time to consider an alley.

The artwork is, through and through, the thing itself. Art, which holds fast to the idea of reconciliation with nature by assuming the processes of nature, is charged with the urge to walk outside of itself. To stop being art. To stop being artificial. To stop being artifice. To be real. Real and viscid and sticky and warm. Poised and natural, the way a head balances on a neck. Turns from left to right. Like an ostrich. Like a cat. Like a man puzzling over a series of dots.

To know what one does not know is not the same as knowing that one does not know what one does not know.

All painting is startling. This is stimulating and sunrise. A formula for the naming of thread. Giant exhibition and oriental splendor. So that there is every hope of an apparition. Convolvulus and dogwood transforming dirt to creamy abstraction. So that it may be said there has been an attempt to formulate an idea, make it palatable and palpable for someone else to revolve and ponder. A utopia. A social realm free of war and bad movies.

How sweet it would be to make music out of one's burdens. To sing oneself into an ecstasy. The fable of time engulfed in a drama of Balearic color.

Is that it, then? Is that the riddle? Or the answer to the riddle?

We are dealing with a very special kind of language here. The language of paint. The language of oil. The language of shape. The language of consistency and texture. The language of density and volume. The language of black. The language of red. The language of blue.

It is, most profoundly and emphatically, a language of blue. The deep blue of the understanding. The blue of the imagination. The blue that dreams of itself as a pull, an attraction, a force on the wall. Something like gravity. But a very frivolous gravity. A gravity in reverse. An anti-gravity. A gravity that makes things float. An antithesis of weight. An antithesis of that which is grave, and engraven. Color in a mode of pure mood. Pure reflection. The colors inside you charged with electric meat. A Balearic octopus crawling its participles across a perception of up. A fable of blue in which a lambent red dagger floats, ready and poised for whatever assassin chooses to slice away the fat of the literal, and enter a realm in which calypso is sung by camellias, and candlewicks blacken in wistful Cordoba.

Blue III. Palma de Mallorca, March 4, 1961.

The thinnest of lines gracefully descends from right to left across the canvas. It is black. It is distinct, consistent in pitch, yet barely perceptible. It is so thin it appears more intuited than seen. It has the weight and consequence of a preposition. Meaning it predicates nothing but space. It is essential to orientation but in no way interferes with the substance of the overall work. It beatifies perception in its delicate beauty. It hangs, drifts, sways in exquisite lightness.

The line in *Blue I* travels diagonally across the canvas, running off the edge at the bottom. This line behaves differently. It moves with a smooth, undulating force, like the tentacle of a deep-sea squid, or the dragline of a spider a light wind has just lifted, and continues to tease.

All around us is an invisible wilderness. Dimensions. Convulsions. Random crystals. The warmth of conviction. Darkness folded into light. Light folded into fury. Lightning slicing the air. King Lear and his fool taking shelter in a hovel. Can a thesis be a flea? I hear an eye. The noise an eye makes is hue. Cathedrals in folds of heavenly blue.

If one follows the line up to the far upper right corner of the canvas one discovers a small patch of red. It has the shape of an oval. It could be a balloon, but it is not a balloon. It could be a kite, but it is not a kite. It is too indeterminate to be the head of a spermatozoid. It is none of these things, yet it suggests all of them. It burns in the corner like a word enkindled with meaning. With neon. With incantation. With the sliver of light that grows into morning.

To the right of the black line is a single black dot. Its placement creates a tension, pulling the eyes to the right when the eyes are simultaneously coaxed to follow the black line to the left. The dot provides no other motive for being. It is simply there. Like a knot, or a swan dive.

It is natural to assume there is a purpose to existence. It is equally natural to assume there is no purpose whatever to existence. Between the poles of this tension is a magnitude of surmise. A lambent need to sprinkle tattoos on the sidewalk. Read Nietzsche in a sidewalk oak. Dress in odysseys of mulch. Reveal the narrative of one's skeleton by walking, swimming, and jumping on a trampoline.

A swan dive is lovely because the body extends into space mocking the tyranny of weight. A leap into space should always be graceful. This is because space gets involved with the eyes like no other occurrence.

Eyes are peculiar things. Organs of sight stuffed with jelly and veins. It is as if blood had a need to see to its wants with the abstract-edness of vision.

Now look again: follow the thin black line toward the bottom of the canvas. As soon as it reaches the far bottom left corner it curls up. It is a gesture of pure caprice.

Engulfing all, swallowing all, absorbing all is that same wonderful blue. Blue, blue, blue. Immediate, immanent, unfathomable.

The simplicity of this painting is Abbevillian. Without its occasional whimsies it would be outright severe. The machinery of its revelation is obvious, but not too obvious. It is the backbone revealed by bending. It is the mystery of concatenation revealed by pythons. Secrets laced with consonants. A thin black line, a big black dot, a bright red oval. And behind it all, rendering it all, a deep sumptuous blue.

A blue so blue it borders on black. A blue so blue it widens the chain of existence to include sticks and knees. A blue so blue it triumphs over the color of death. A blue so blue it is natural and alive, a piece of heaven squeezed out of a tube and applied smoothly and evenly to the surface of a canvas. So that it creates a domain of possibility. A smudge, a smear, a dot. A thin black line and an unmade bed. The smell of paint with a whiff of thinner in the background. An extended arm, and a daub of red.

EVE'S MEDIUM

for Eve Ascheim

Eve's paintings were opera, music teeming with intimation. The faces I brought with me were dust. I only mention that because one's private thoughts are always inimitable and cruise the mind like alchemy and glucose. Eve's feeling for space was huge, but the fainter lines made it appear soft as woodwinds, a feeling of patterns shuttled back and forth on a loom, swift, light, assiduously impromptu. Eve said she did not listen to music when she worked. Anyone who has ever played in an orchestra knows that the space inside music is a solitary gaze. Blisters prove that a diary written in a free hand is a story tangled in our personal meat. The voices at the opera are huge, but how do we reproduce them in silence? When a small bell is jingled the staircase appears more helical. Why is that? Is it because thunder is loudest in wood? Is it because taut strings thrill with decision? Time is experimental, but space assists the shape of the piano. Italian and French always amaze me when they are juggled like chlorophyll. The Renaissance abounds in perspective. Even a fire crackles with shape. We can see it in Rembrandt making light and civilization. After a moment of silence, we heard a voice coming out of a woman's head. She was asking a question about Eve's medium. Did she use pencil or charcoal? Anything, said Eve. The answer was soothing, and frank. I felt a quiet emotion burgeon into a brilliant darkness. Everything was a silence, a lush philosophy chiseled out of air. Artifacts of breath floating radius and pi.

Moulin Bleu

Consider a mill. Consider it blue. Consider a disarray of tools that are rusting in dew. Consider the force of a current. Consider a daily saga of creaking gears. Wild English words in a tumult of provocation. The greenhouse begins to climb its glass. The drum is one part drum one part acetaminophen. Geyser means it is roan and possibly Icelandic to brave the semantics of ruin with anything but the hilt of a word in your throat. The monsters on the boulevard will each banana that bang you call a wildcat. The vice of poetry inheres in each of us and each of us must turn it to a virtue that brawls among our ribs like an emotion intervening between earth and heaven. Be grass. Be chaos. Be chaos on the grass. Be chaos, grass. Negligee what's negligent and cram what is crimson with hats. Surgically, it resembles a telescope removed from a word still dripping with miniskirts. The buckskin feels like an occurrence of clothes gone into total indulgence. Worn, soft, seasoned. The intrinsic part of garnering gems for the diadem of day. We shall crown that salamander with the moraine that is Messiaen. And call it a day and go home. Indulge indigo, my friend. It will occur to you one day to cube that contusion on your arm and brace it in bubbles. A cloud of pain will drool down your sides like the tongue of a dinosaur. The surf is fricative with frolic, a contagion of salt and foam the sand just swallows with natural abandon. The ethereal rug we weave with our words is mostly spit. This concerns everyone. Because the beatitude of blood might be orchestrated in a book. An eyeball I charm with eddies of glaze and fathom. How graceful everybody is during the noise of their lives. Have you ever seen grace in the glow of neon? Was it red, or blue? A hive of such waxy abstraction ratchets up this conjecture to the force of a deck chair, exalts it to the level of mumbling until it can assume itself to be a sequence of words. Knead it with need. Murmur it with heraldry and bolts. There is a gamut to this preserved in negativity. A hydrogen painting instinctively brushed with a cake bone on Saturday. The gourmands recommended such intertwining as an inducement to taste whatever necessity emerges from the throat in the form of a moan, a groan with a beard. A tendency pitched in vellum with illuminations of bullfrog and mill.

TREMBLING GOBBETS OF LANGUAGE

How do you sew a pound
of accretion to the sound
of a needle of a noun? Thread it with a string
of explosions, Balinese

puppets & the collateral
of a throat clicking out of the lung
of an emotion

made of rain. As Artaud's Theatre of Cruelty
doubled & redoubled in brightness, Ed Sullivan
walked out on the stage, vigorously shaking

Antonin's hand & smiling. An alphabet
of light danced around his teeth. Riding
a rocket is a thrill & I love it
said the astronaut
to the incendiary

of a diphthong. There is oil
in the coil

of the wind said the curtain
of oolitic oolong. It is a powwow
of many carbonating throats. Reality
gathers in places like London
& ciliates across the wire like a thread

of color. A large gloomy cloud
bending the light into a jaw
of algebra. Identity
is something you wear. It looks
like a cecropia moth

with a crepuscular mouth. Trembling
gobbets of language. You can take the moth
out of the mouth but you cannot take the music
out of the musk ox. Belief
is an abstraction, like soap. Adumbrations
of profligate air, blueprints
& handsprings, revelations

like roads. If television were a thumb
it would finger words
like foliage & grip
the eyes at the roots
of possibility. Incidents of marble
prolong the interview
with Andy Warhol. He had a grip

on oblivion. This is why I became a poet. I wanted to be
seven stomachs & a mouth of steam.

MERCURY

In the form of cinnabar, mercury is a bright red, a blood-like element found near hot springs and in low-temperature veins, typically near volcanic rocks. It may also be found as silvery globules in deposits of cinnabar.

A metal, it behaves more like a liquid. Its Latin name is *hydrargyrus.*

Water-silver. Silver-water.

I broke a thermometer on a hospital floor once, where I was working as a messenger, and a blob of mercury rolled out. It was tempting to pick it up and roll it around in my hand, but I was warned not to. It is a metal. It can kill. It will weight your blood with elemental logic. It will translate you. It will grasp you like sugar and haunt you like a laboratory of nouns.

Mercury is a messenger. It brings messages of spirit. This makes it ideal for barometers and thermometers, as if of all metals mercury were the only one sensitive enough to register such slight aberrations as temperature and atmospheric pressure, the only metal approximating the human condition, rising and falling with the temperature of a social circumstance.

Rising and falling with the weight of a problem, the pressure of a situation.

A duel in the winter of 1772.

A revelation by a painter on a Tahitian island in 1902.

Rainbow swirls of color soaked into the sidewalk by the cemetery.

Mercury makes light.

The Mercury-arc lamp is a fused quartz tube full of confined mercury. When a current is passed through it the metal vaporizes, like a thought, giving a greenish-blue luminescence.

Mercury is malleable and bright. It is a word, like any other word, only brighter, sometimes a violet pulling on blue, a spurt of metal from a fever near the equator.

➤

The lips go together to make the 'm,' then burst apart to form the first vowel sound, an ur sound, the sound of allure, of something dangerous and bright. A syllable. A myrrh. A word rolled out of the night.

Restrictions Unbound

One may not mail blank
invoices to Costa Rica, nor manufactured
and unmanufactured platinum, dual-gradation
feeding bottles, or flammable or explosive

substances. One may not mail aluminum
foil for tobacco manufacturing to Greece
or firearms or swords. Fresh meat, preserved meat,
rawhides, wool, and other animal products
must be accompanied by a certificate
showing the place of origin and stating it is free

of disease. Perishable confectionary
is prohibited to Mexico, as are pistols
and other devices for emitting tear gas.
Chocolate and products made of chocolate
require prior authorization
from the Mexican Secretary of Commerce.
One may not mail horror

comics to Britain, or obscene
articles, prints, paintings, cards,
films, videotapes, etc. Seal
skins and switchblade knives
are also prohibited, as are cards
decorated with mica or ground glass.
The postmaster will refuse to accept
parcels containing honeybees

for Canada, unless they bear
such endorsement. Queen bees
are not subject to the above restriction.
Chad will not accept fish, vegetables and plums

bearing in large type
the mark of origin, or contained in tins
weighing less than 1 kilogram, but butane
gas lighters and refills, harpoons and spear guns

used for undersea fishing may not
be mailed to Malaysia. An individual
in Romania may receive gift parcels

up to a total weight of 55 pounds per year.
Paper and writing products, envelopes,
ink, pencils, pens, erasers, chalk, etc.
may not be sent to Sri Lanka
though banknotes will be permitted to Portugal
if the addressee has a license
issued by the Bank of Portugal.
St. Lucia will not accept shaving

brushes made in Japan
and articles of silk
chessboards, tapestries, lace, and chemical
dyes that are not sufficiently fast
for dyeing wool carpets may not

go to Afghanistan.
Hay and straw and articles made of straw
may not be sent to Ireland, nor safety
fuses and fireworks. Peat moss
litter is permitted if under license.
Margarine, skimmed milk, and other diluted
or adulterated foodstuffs must be suitably labeled.
American cotton, arms, ammunition, coffee

plants, coffee seeds, coffee beans
and hemp may not be sent to Bangladesh
nor piece goods ordinarily sold by the yard
or by the piece manufactured outside Bangladesh
nor quinine, colored pink.

CONTRABASSOON

The convolution of the contrabassoon
functions as a marsh
in the orchestra of the sun, an expansive
smear of Shakespeare. The very problem

of a relationship between bubble and verb
betrays a metaphysics of presence
and embouchure, this word

here for instance is a balloon
inflated with breath, and Shakespeare
understood the syntax of nature, the way it drifts
or boils out of vapor

making thunder. The contrabassoon
on the other hand achieved
a greater practicability in metal
which could be folded in any desired form
generally a tube of hardwood with a bore of variable taper
somewhat more acute

than the oboe. Sometimes a sound
will seem irrational as brass
in a pond of remembrance, air
hammered into a sonnet

of incandescence and twine. There are some arabesques
I'd like to show you as well, automobile
door handles rippling with Dutch
mannerist coral, the roar
of a busy pen yodeling silt

and subjectivity. Imagination
adorns the lettuce as lettuce adorns
the dirt. How beautiful

in bloom as a contrabassoon
throbbing with franchise
is a hole in the head

for giving advice. Advice is good
but a contrabassoon, a contrabassoon

is a sound. It is the sound
of the contrabassoon. It is not the sound
of sand, or the sand

of the measure of sound
or blood being drawn or doors sliding shut
It is the bound of the apothegm of onions

It is the noon of the onion

It is the sound of the contrabassoon.

BAGPIPE

A drone from a bag of tassels
is shaped by amazing
grace. It's a weird thing
a bag of plaid bristling with pipes
you can feel the wool of it by looking at it
but the sound eludes
invention, it adheres

to the water tumbling over the rocks
like custom esthetics, the ceramics of stress
or gazing at a pail of milk
as daybreak heaves its hulk
and opera over the hills

of Scotland, which is ingested
from curbs in Edinburgh or Eriskey
and the drone of the bagpipes
oscillating like ice
or a tongue licking the cream
from a cherry
held together by molecules

and conciliatory horseshoes
the boiling distinction of an outboard
purring on a lake at dawn
or the drone

of an unvarying A
beneath the melodies fingered on the chanter

for the piquancy of the pipes
among deep green hills
as dripping water hollows a stone

so the writing of poetry
can build a neck of snow
and cliffs and sea

burning with voices
in the underlying rocks, an enormous
music magnetic as words. You might say
a bagpipe is a primordial accordion
fueling the spirit of a strathspey

experienced by the agreement of the senses
as roses, or barrels of fish
a general hopefulness
awakening the drone of the pipes
to fountain diamonds of sound
and perchance the weight of poets
a wheel of granite for sharpening knives.

RED GUITARS

One wants to reach up & scoop the stars
into wax. The black thread

of a yellow idea. Sparks whirling out of the fire
if it doesn't end, it is just

organized around the snow
like water. One day I came

to consider the day as a bucket of words
Whatever you say makes a world

but it is premature to kiss the geisha
or give a speech

to the men & women settling the wilderness
for the cultivation of wheat

bread & a ladle of daylight
curling over the tongue

in a beguiling gulp
of prolegomenon. Ideas

are to literature what light is to painting
the harvest of a quiet eye

attached to the hood of a car
like an open G

tuning on a metallic red
guitar. The habit of skin

as repose. Coleridge holds
that a man cannot have a pure mind

who refuses apple dumplings. A nipple
in the mouth, or fipple or flute

spewing gobbets of music
while the pronouns walk around

clicking with participles. Clicking
because it is a clicking world. Crackling

because it is a moving colluvium of magmas & tars
If magmas cool beneath the surface they form camellias

of iron. If magmas cool beneath the surface they spit
& wheeze. They hiss. They whistle. They sizzle like red
guitars.

XYLOPHONE

listening to Berlioz
I feel that energy

of the dishwasher
is different
than the infrared logic of the xylophone
which is a skeleton of the piano
it is lackadaisical to realize this
snow on the rake

might be pulled through grooves of music
as the notes of the bars of the xylophone
in Saint-Saens' *Dans Macabre*
enhance the baggage of the stars
tone is a stick

of dark blue with a fringe of red
at the bottom, and rose. Powder
metallurgy is ideal for making steel
and brass sockets (toothed parts)
and cams (grooves parts) but a xylophone
is a vertebrae

of inflections, an undulating
sound of elegant clarity
and meat, the naked thirst of color
wiggling in the dark like a tongue
of silver hit with a hammer

to produce a contour
of insubordinate spangles
the wit in the distillate
of ingots of sounds
a hive of bells

➤

pollinating rhythm
and beryllium

beaten into rain.

Prose Sonata In G-Flat

Music is a dimension of memory and mode. The notion that certain effects of music are so much like feelings that we mistake them for flashlights is illuminating. Imagine enamel. Impersonate yeast. Music baked in solitude appeases the pain of romance. It awakens the soul. It is a raft of sound floating in the air like a fact cracked into pine.

Music articulates the forms that language cannot set forth, like slowly getting into a hot bath, or feeling the current of a river pull against your legs.

Music is an essence of scale. It is a graduation of treasures beyond the world.

Music is the water lapping the sand of foreign shores, chromatic tones touching the ivory of incorporeal dominions. Blocks of sound gliding up and down. Hammers pounding pandemonium on string.

Words scar the air like a reptile immersed in Mozart. Skin heaving tongues of wet trembling sound.

A piece of music can embody a feeling a debut of doubt a triumph of will a man sitting at a table pondering a fragrance.

Space hemorrhaging thunder. Snow somersaulting in a glass wound. Shakespeare crackling with sonnets. Being and nothingness mingled in dots.

Music is made by instruments, oboes, pianos, violins, and clarinets. The world of sound is constructed with percussion and tone, melody and bone. Thelonius Monk leaning into a keyboard to draw sounds out of rosewood and contiguity.

The native hue of resolution is immaterial. Perceptions render the world accessible to thought. Top hats and chandeliers. Jets and blackberries. The savor of fugitive phenomena. The play of fingers on a keyboard. A nuance percolating through stone. A cobweb floating in a borderland between keys.

The shadows between notes widen with undulation. The lights and shadows between notes trace implications of a space haunted by portent and otherworldly phenomena. The cold edge of the abyss. Impressionist paintings on the walls. Meaning is thick when it spills an emotion. Piccolos, pianos, drums. Violins creating elusive effects. In such instances we are being led by the ears towards a knowledge of the human heart. Ermine and art. Energy and stars.

The play of lights and shadows deepen a consonant twisted to sound like quartz. A watercolor fantasia welcomes the interval of a perfect fifth. There is no single emotion that cannot be splattered with flutes.

The life of a pin or a mood rippling with vespers deepens the hyacinths reflected on the surface of a pond. The pop and crackle of a fire in a stone hearth walks the walls between notes. Saturn's rings provides the raw material of sound pulse of an inner spirit not one but many human emotions harps and the human voice ribs, blood, heart, spleen, bladder, bones, muscles, circulation light prismatically broken into separate colors those quiet browns in a painting by Rembrandt art is not a material place but a non-place stars trembled by the handshake of gravity a veiled blending of hues a sound sliding down a closet door.

Music comes from the body the blaze of white in new fallen snow daylight nailed to a nerve circumnavigation of the tonal globe in an invisible realm. A G-flat descending to F elucidates a photograph of deer. Evanescent harmonies breathe a blend of emotions into an otherworldly domain vapor dangled in knots flutes and clarinets in the dark lower register. A box of laundry detergent vivified at noon by a ray of sunlight.

Humanism means headlights, the crucial ingredients of a conviction. There is a music for that, too, and it comes from the din of traffic, cantatas of gas and combustion.

But there are worlds not so immediate as ours. Not so decisive as a sidewalk. A school of smelt just below the surface of the sound of a sound surrenders the invisible made visible to the ears gravity and ointment violins in their lustrous upper range a railroad redeemed by melody the give in a trampoline a thesis of light in search of a prism a sonata crowded with meaning the heart teeming with feeling.

A music born of words is like an earthquake folded into a harp a raw tone of nervous beauty copper pipes zinc counters a stretch of air ribboned with larks the muscle of proposition lifting a volume of tints and crickets.

Characters in Proust are unzipped by music a cymbal brushed with drumsticks arouses the smell of popcorn in a movie theatre busy words huddled in ink shapes shells columns vaults a gladiator entering the ring embossed wings on a Roman shield.

A realism consistent with horses gravity described by carrots might be twisted into winter. Thus music has fulfilled its mission whenever the voice pours out of the head in gleaming overtures of pitch and portulaca.

The writer as musician the painter as a phantom amid a uniform gray a shape taking form in the light the diffusion of tints in the cream of clarinets. The baroque organ had a transparent tone that was oftentimes absorbed in angora. Preludes, nocturnes, arabesques. Feelings are genuine it is words that sometimes fail us. The biography of a crowbar explains the failure of the human face to topple the tyranny of the eyebrow.

Pain is a tool. We can use it to make contrast, history, heaviness and sauerkraut. The creaking floor of a tool shed a rubber tongue bouncing an alphabet of bees.

A bright silver tone captures the feeling of hindsight, the mathematics of apology aching with moonlight. A leaning toward an intimate lyricism that evokes worn leather wallets and faucets, a steam radiator in an old hotel. A closet crowded with ghosts. The disorganization of vision. Down is up upside down.

A truck parked by a diner in Oregon grips the residue of experience and gives it the tender, subtle, intimate expression of grease and oil, the mysteries of diesel and the music of gears. Insects attracted by sugar. Slammed screen doors. An ambient western charm that has allowed room for so many personalities that life assumes the calm reflections of an idle digression, an oar in the water dragging behind the stern of a small boat. Aberration in all its forms. Strange, unexpected radio stations picked up late at night while on the road. Clouds scudding past the moon. Static. Headlights. Outburst. And then, finally, that piece of music you have waited your entire life for, its sounds are so alluring, so familiar, yet so unfamiliar, haunting and glad.

Words are tinctured with music so that we may give titles to fables, haze on West Virginia hills, the curl of leaves and flowers, a bell tinkling on a gate. A world of dream and enchantments, fountains in fonts, the clatter of tools in a toolbox.

Space is the music of volume, a man holding a detour sign by a road crew. All around us are invisible chambers, consonant chords overlaid with dissonant intervals. A chair moved closer to a window. People in skins and helmets. Trout swimming under a branch of cedar.

Tone combinations are French as bread, gardens in the rain, circumference jangly with bells. There results a fluid scale pattern large as all life, the clash of overtones on a piece of cardboard someone has used to paint a room multiple colors, the paint dripping and dribbling with random inevitability, like the black in Pollock's *Sea Change* igniting the reds and silvers, little daubs of blue, like the rumble of a dryer accented with the occasional clicks of metal snaps and the clatter of commingled zippers.

It's like that. Always like that. A music not quite squeezed into the words. So that it cries for a sunrise. Rhetoric erratic as a bat.

Ra ium →

Fine needle point
on which is shown
a small particle of
Radium, just a few
atoms, which are
quite invisible to
even the highest
magnifying power

MORNING ARRIVAL

I feel a devotion to the story, to the divulgence of faucets and
neutrons, the train of sunrise and mathematical milk. The train of
ruggedness brooding in the metals of history. The train of snow with .
its blobs of light and problems of consciousness. Its unwieldy flowers
humped with beauty. Its entanglements and shoes. Its nostalgia for
childhood. Its chug and decorations. Its oils. Its sparkling ideas of
napkins and narcotic remembrances of mint. The train of surmise the
train of going deep underground. The train full of left arms and
blades of perception. The train of glass smashed into premonition.
The train of consonants. The train of curtains the train of dreams the
train of rebukes and washing machines. The train of pianos and
conceptions of mink. The train of nesting in the stratosphere. The
train of almanacs aroused by infinite shanks of present tense talking
to the wind with a mouth of fire.

There is a sound attached to the word "curtain" that causes it to
guarantee mahogany. Everyone on the train knows this. Everyone on
the train feels rustic. Everyone on the train is snapping a picture.
Everyone on the train is a pure invention of taffeta and ore. Everyone
on the train is built out of water. Everyone on the train is sleeping
among facts of scallop and volume. Everyone is a prodigal wonder.
Everyone invokes the luscious architecture of fog piping a radical
disease of eyes to the lurid resolution of an orange. The orange is an
incalculable assessment of juice. The orange is buckled to the humidi-
ty of an utterance ripening in hawthorn. The orange is a symbol of
beauty. The orange is socially constructed. The orange is peeled and
ready for the garbage. The orange orange. The marvelous orange. The
orange aboard the train. The orange train. The train of oranges. The
train of a single orange of polychromatic temperature. The orange on
its way to Boise. The orange on its way to Kennewick. The orange on
its way to Massapequa. The orange in its lantern of prose. The orange
in its hypotenuse of sexual juice.

Below us a river curves into a bruise of iridescent blue. An imper-
tinent plausibility of time plumps itself into a translucent artifact of

space. Auxiliaries of verbal undulation pull the train into the chill of morning. The train arrives. The train is arriving. The train is arriving in constellations of bulk and compression. Here is the train. There is the train. This is the train. This is an orange. This is an orange and this is a train. The caribou are gratuitous. The caribou are soft as the present tense of a pork chop. The caribou are unfolding from the day like a hill. The caribou are giving you an image of caribou. The pitch of space in a bulb of volume. The apoplectic assumption of a fish bouncing down the street.

I Was An Extra On Gunsmoke

I was an extra on *Gunsmoke*. I played words. Sometimes rain. Sometimes a big noise like a plate breaking on the floor of the Long Branch.

Once I burned in a lamp making a crude room taste belligerent, like a belly full of buckwheat, or a brain full of thought. Matt Dillon told me to calm down and write a sonnet. Gunplay leads to blood and machinery. We will not have any talk of revolution in Dodge. Matt's voice was heavy as architecture. It felt like a bank falling through me. I felt coins of wisdom on my bones, and money in my consonants, making them lapidary, and jingly.

Some of you may remember that *Gunsmoke* was an important series of allegories every week that taught us how to be noble and dig deeper into life's meaning. Paragraphs of straw helped the stable into instability, while elsewhere leaves of oak and elm nibbled the light of the Kansas horizon.

Amanda Blake took me aside and said my money was welcome but she didn't want any trouble. She loved animals, and kept leopards in her backyard. I always wondered if that mole on her cheek was real, or just a curious allusion to seventeenth century France, and the court at Versailles, within a western context. Her performances were always right on. It seemed as if running a saloon were a truer occupation than her life as an actress. This was evident in her carriage. And the Rembrandt hanging above her escritoire.

Doc sat down for a beer. He was always fatigued and grouchy, tired of seeing life come into this world just to die. I generally kept out of his way.

Chester was on hand for comic relief. One afternoon he went out in back of the jail with a piece of plywood and painted a most wonderful abstraction of paste and gunpowder titled "Section."

"Section of what," said Doc.

"Daylight," said Chester, lighting it on fire.

Chester was always doing odd things around the jail when Marshal Dillon was away arresting people or trying to persuade them to behave more kindly to one another or he would have to kill them.

Dillon was always avoiding fights but getting into them anyway because men were constantly testing his mettle. This gave *Gunsmoke* tragic significance. This gave *Gunsmoke* its dimension of existential thirst and ethical ambiguity. Its yeast and leaven. Its slice of life.

Occasionally my artistry as an extra was challenged. I can handle footprints, I told the director one day, but the solar sister of art must be turned gently, like a speed. Footprints have to be coaxed into this world like everything else, or they'll end up looking like valentines in a probability vector. You don't want Marshal Dillon tracking a troop of truculent trombonists.

He told me footprints are traces of peripatetic endeavor, not holes in the earth hemorrhaging boulders.

One day the ambassador of a skeleton came to town selling a hot red energy in a bottle. I was fragments that day, a farm on the outskirts of town, more memory than popcorn, though sometimes I had to play the wing nuts as well. Hardware was indiscriminate in those days, indicative of a kind of fugitive pragmatism inserted into the script for its flavor of authenticity and timber meeting the ore of a mythological west.

We used language and song to honor the barns. There was delft in some of the kitchens, and figs and Icelandic sagas among the immigrants. Doorjambs signified sorority, the deep distress sometimes masquerading as experience. The smell of actual gun smoke eluded most of the TV audience, but it was there, fully evident in our actual nostrils. Our words were bullets. Our bullets were words. Bullets and words immersed in action, the beautiful acrimony of the impending duel, the somber racket of the poolroom.

I sometimes got to fraternize with the bandits, but I was careful not to seem too explicit, or experimental. They were easily riled. All they understood was guns and money. Dice and cards in the studio cafeteria.

Yes I was an extra on *Gunsmoke*. Though nothing was ever really extra on *Gunsmoke*. Not the smoke, not the guns, not the horses, not the dust. Not even Kansas, which was a fiction larger than Kansas, which is itself a fiction, a state, a way of being. Dodge was named Dodge because everything, ultimately, is a diversion. A plate of succotash, or the diversity of opinion concerning fish.

CAPTAIN NEMO SERVES
PROFESSOR ARONNAX

Captain Nemo serves professor Aronnax
tortue de mer, foies de dauphin & confitures

d'anémones. Meanwhile above
the water enclosing the outer

hull the breakers roll in & crash
on the shores of Tahiti & the Nautilus

unravels its meanings in octo-
syllables & tumultuous vowels

blown into opals with fins & mouths
just like a real poem. Can a purpose

be suggested for luminescence
in cephalopods? A complete answer

cannot be given because the deep-sea
habitat of most luminescent squid

makes direct observation
almost impossible. Jules Verne

wrote a number of books of science
fiction & later gave birth

to Raymond Roussel. Oysters
& mussels, syntax

& *forêts sous-marines.* Octopi can crawl
through almost unbelievably small

openings. To reach a desirable lair
an octopus will flatten its rubbery body

& ooze through a hole several times
smaller than the diameter of its body

Je n'étais pas le maître de mes paroles
confessed Paul Eluard at the window

of the real. The necessity of speaking
& the desire not to be heard. The meaning

in a motion & the meaning between
the meaning. A larger view of things

at the bottom or the top or the in-between
the solemn geography of human limits

like the eye of the Nautilus
opening on the bottom of the ocean.

ALPHABET SOUP

The language of the gene is an idiom of soup. It is a syntax of ooze and adaptation. It is a broth of spirals. It is an alphabet of meat.

The genetic language has an alphabet of 4 letters. A, G, C and T. Adenine, guanine, cytosine and thymine. Four letters with 64 permutational possibilities. Four letters for creating gorillas and egrets and barracudas. Four chemicals for creating lilacs and caribou.

Imagine sunlight on a puddle of algal goop. Imagine this algal goop shaping 141 amino acids into a red blood protein.

Imagine protein.

Imagine goop.

The imagination you're using to imagine the protein and goop was once protein and goop. Is still largely protein and goop.

This is about protein.

This is about goop.

Bright luminous veins of startling light veining the methane of the primordial atmosphere, chemicals stirred by lightning into huge Proustian sentences and furious velvet leaves.

If DNA is a ladder, than the nucleotide is a rung. It is the rung that contains the code for replicating itself into a camel or octopus, leopard or baritone.

It is the number of rungs in the ladder, the number of hips in a tango, the number of orchids in a jungle that determines what the twisting, turning, tangled chain of amino acids are going to produce. The sequencing of parts determines the whole, as syntax determines the flavor of a sentence, or the universal rhythms governing plant growth determine the shape of a leaf or the coil of a tendril, as clavicles determine clavichords and clavichords determine touch, as keys determine locks and locks determine keys. As walks determine fugues and fugues determine walks.

It is the order of the amino acids that make up the rungs, that make a warm autumn burning patterns of gold in the leaves, a woman bundled in wool getting into a cab in New York.

➤

The sequencing of proteins produces silk and decorum, fractal objects, cartilage and orchids.

DNA makes another cell by dividing into convictions and friends, Fibonacci spiral pairs, and theories and signatures.

The molecule is a long and irregularly arranged sequence of amino acids, like an irregularly arranged string of colored beads, tree roots, tributaries, lightning. Conspicuous tendrils travel into renown and bells and wrists. Chromosomes shorten and thicken into bighorn and blondes, primrose and woodsmen, magnets and currency. An enzyme then completes the synthesis of the complementary strands in a ceremony of violent consonance and brutal harmony.

Various enzymes are used to unlock and unwind the double helix, so that thresholds of new being may be crossed, so that DNA fragments may combine to produce thrashed water in a hatchery, fins and scales and the geometry of growth may be renewed and carried into veins on a leaf, echoes in a government hall, the lights and bustle of a Reno casino.

The chromosomes unwind back into invisibility as somewhere in a half-finished aluminum equipment shed spermatozoa swim toward the heavy liquids of fate and living forms.

A single gene is a group of instructions, and in the nonlinear dynamics of chaos a swarm of genes become a nomadic flotilla whose coding is carried in the rungs and yardarms of the DNA molecule, the tongues and legs of future generations, the steam of yesterday's rain in the tread of today's tractor, a new intermingling and palette of possibilities.

Nature uses accident and diversity to arrive at shapes with the least resistance to wind and water. Nature incorporates the noble numbers in the public epoxy, a doll within a doll within a doll, twigs and salamanders and lunatic basement phantoms.

Several themes flow through life one of which is passionate and mystical while the other is sticky and lewd.

The DNA molecule divides into kites of lambent destiny, spirals and squawks of seagull joy, chromosomes dangling in the wind, sunlight splashed on a memory of water. Electricity and footsteps unleash the poetry within, okra, papaya, gallons of obsidian hunger and the Fibonacci spiral pairs singing "Mr. Tambourine Man."

The precise order of words along the chromosome indicate the order of amino acids making up a particular protein, a muscle or fin, enzyme or sentient being full of testosterone and pulp. The aptitude for geography or augury or convening a parliamentary assembly originates in a molecule inside the nucleus of each cell.

Nerve cells form a fabric called skin, which is a parchment or membrane on which may be written a destiny or wrinkle, mermaid or anchor.

Club cars and Micmac attest to the diversity of protein synthesis, which is a process known as translation. A gene might be translated in a wildly colorful tie selected one day on a trip to Milwaukee, or stamp collecting or golf.

Most values or truths coveted by writing are out of reach of mammals and lizards who are mostly involved in differentiation, like chickens scattered in a barnyard or the furious genetic struggle of a structure in turmoil to communicate a bottle or long bar of soap.

The sympathy of a warm snout might be expressed in the basal layer of epidermis on one's fingers or toes, or an echo stitched to the horn of a mechanical skeleton.

Deoxyribonucleic acid is a direct cab to the destinations and catastrophes of our lives, the velvet of our daily reverie.

Hematopoietic stem cells may have nonredundant roles in the delights bubbling from the personality of my shirt, but who is to know if the molecule of a local impulse flows through my thinking like the levity of a regal autumn afternoon.

Poetry is a universe of enactments. DNA is a universe of spirals.

Each gene is a spiral of proteins forming chains of illimitable association, blood and conversation, eyeballs and valleys. This effect requires direct cell-to-cell contact among dogs and poplars. The nucleus is a furnace in which a human being emerges like a loaf of brain or screenplay. Every moment yields genes that are differentially expressed, that remain images through the delineation of outlines and the viscera of throats disturbed by words, that leap from being to being by the language of genetics which is a tale of two cities told in cells, which is conveyed in the elegant crystallographic x-ray photographs of Rosalind Franklin, provocative and steaming like a postcard from Hamlet.

The letters of the Roman alphabet let a maelstrom of meaning consent to the flight of cattle in much the same way a passionate protein will unleash a double helix of delirious seeds, torrential neurotransmitters deciphering and filtering the realities of a normal existence in the embryos of fruit flies, or flat stones arranged on the ground somewhere west of Kansas City.

Stromal fibroblasts do not a painted garden make, not without a brush and a complicated boulevard of double-stranded molecules winding themselves around in seemingly endless spirals, each one unzipping itself down the middle to form two separate strands of writing which will join in a recombinant delirium of diphthongs and dugongs and oak. A dollop of daydream on a yellow background of Brazilian rubber trees.

Writing is trying always to find more about the essence of writing, the substance of epoxy and the mystery of personality. Genes initiate this moss with spit and literality. The entire alphabet of the genetic language is simple as a bowl of sparkling vichyssoise, the reality of wilderness in cell fate decisions unzipping and zipping themselves into hips and ribs and ankles and hands, into fins and lips and fascicles of epidermal fiber.

It is stunning how a muslin of future narration might bind to the cytoplasmic domains or an epicure might be born in a malapropism one day in Alabama with a banyan on his knee.

The biology of the umbilical cord is profuse with electrochemical information and blood. Candlelight, bistros, and wax. Bass, piano, and sax.

It takes twenty amino acids to describe the silk of paradise. Chromosomes and sparkling sugars. Four letters. A, G, C, and T. Adenine, cytosine, guanine, and tinsel on a Jetta spiraled around the ski racks.

MY FAVORITE GLAND

A gland is an organ that extracts specific substances from the blood and concentrates or alters them for subsequent secretion.

How can anyone not love a gland?

A pool makes swimming genial and Rilke. A gland makes saliva generous and available. A gland makes everything groovy. There is a gland for land and walking on land and zigzags and drama. There is a gland for metaphors and a gland for putting existence before banjos. There is a gland for wounds and a gland for buttes and flutes and drumsticks and warts. There is a gland for digestion and suggestion and translucence and sweat.

A ball of ganglia harvests the sky. A gland surrounds it with wrinkles and sand.

There is a gland in the head and a gland in the hand. There is a gland that incarnates sentiment and makes it Saturday and demonstrable. There is a gland that secretes hormones and a gland that secretes Calypso and Kickapoo and screwdrivers and eggs.

The pituitary gland is a lobed structure, less than half an inch in diameter, that hangs from the floor of the brain by a stalk, the infundibulum. How can anyone not love a gland that hangs from a stalk called an infundibulum?

Personally I prefer Spain. The light squirts out of a big ball in the sky making blood and roller skates.

The body is an aggregate of numerous glands.

My favorite gland is the one that triggers estrogen.

My favorite gland is an alphabet provoking the naked holes of Tuesday.

My favorite gland is experience.

My favorite gland is a closet full of cloth and rubber.

To be is an instinct. Not to be is a frost.

Ink is a secretion of writing.

My favorite gland is a preposition. A preposition twists the window into Philadelphia. A preposition secretes Technicolor sequences of attitude and bearing. A preposition hangs from the floor of the brain by a stalk called a pronoun.

Flags are glands on poles flapping and flapping and clacking and cloth.

A warm transparent supernatural glass indicates a gland of grammar and verbal construction.

Thank you for reading about glands. Thank you for thinking about glands.

Identity is a product of the gland for hope and chimeras.

Aesthetics continues the gland of muscularity.

The volcano is a gland of fire and molten rock.

The gland of sorrow secretes a mechanical cow.

There is no use in finding out what is in anyone's glands you will find out soon enough that a postage stamp spurts borders.

You will find a floodlight in your mouth secreting illumination. You will find a breath in your words that makes them rumble with gabardine and cycads. You will find a gland in your gingham exemplifying genitalia. You will find a brutal ghost of hair on your head and think it is a memory of syllables.

Semen says see the men.

Semen says cement the men.

Semen says see some women persist in conjugation.

My favorite gland sparkles among the evergreens.

This is the time to say that a government is crisp when it grants mercury and galleries and hallucinates democracy among the rich.

My favorite gland secretes dimes and diameter and dialogue and iron.

It is the helium of everything.

It is what is knightly.

It is what is intricate and hot with life.

It tastes like sunlight.

Curiosity Was Born With The Universe

Curiosité naquît avec l'universe.
—Le Comte de Lautréamont

Yesterday's rain led to accordion clouds, freakish testaments of moisture. Today a band of lavender pools in a basin of quadrilateral mint, hinting at endless churning colors regenerating the skin of logic on a glockenspiel.

We invent words to shoot lightning, and this is what we call regret.

What we need is tape and ribbon. Ineffability and plain human concern.

Sometimes I see William Blake riding a pinto into eternity. And sometimes I see a woman's nipple in a universe of elves.

I know it's there. I can hear it when I walk.

Later, when we returned to the VCR, I made the sperm go backward. The chemistry of assault conceives a great black juice of heaving pleasure. As every passion has its proper pulse, the granite balloon of a phenomenal ambiguity rises from a gummed label and pops.

Shards of intellectual endeavor fall to the ground in flames.

The average cow is a perfect example of breath. Incidents of skin and amplitude. Pigment and horn. Cylinders and grass.

Curiosity was born with the universe. Curiosity did not kill the cat. Boredom killed the cat. Curiosity redeems the monotony of the rotor. Curiosity cures fiction. Curiosity fountains the architecture of names.

Curiosity is curious and sneezes morphine. Curiosity is erotic and involves fluids. Curiosity is dreamy as stars, a curiously round sentence of zigzags and quail. Hepatica and autumn. The interior of the sun. The mystery of dirt porcelain and bingo incidents of rail.

The inevitable genitalia of a metropolitan owl.

City of Water

I live in a city of water. Water in all its forms. Vapor, clouds, drizzle. Fountains, rivers, lakes. Inlets, ports, sounds. There is water everywhere. Water has shaped and bathed and baffled the city. There is water to drink and water to boil. Water glittering and deep. Water glittering and wide. Water quivering and radiant and sympathetic to the philosophy of immersion. Water turquoise and green. Water with the complexion of smoldering topaz. Water to break water to wash water to enact in Elizabethan costume. Water to map water to absorb water to arrange with tubs and names. Duwamish. Shilshole. Sammamish. Water permeable as Beethoven and convincing as mud. Wherever you go in the city you cannot escape it. You can only surrender to the fact of it. The ubiquity of it. Its omnipresence and moss. Water parceled in berries. Water full of nuance and mallards and waves. Water in bogs. Water in bags. Water in guns. Water squirted into the face. Water under pressure water circulating a labyrinth of pipes. Water filtered through faucets water adjusted in nozzles. Water tumbled in the mind in images of rock and convulsion. Water in my body. Water around my body. Water in spit water in thumbs and eyeballs. Water punctuating the earth with commas. Puddles promiscuous as nickels. Puddles impertinent as pickles. Water streaked with whorls of delinquent oil. Everywhere the sheen and luster of water. Rivers in reveries of water. Water pushed to extremes. Water falling from cliffs. Water sprayed over melons. Water in beads on the blade of a fern. Water in rivulets on a window. Water impelling a current water moving in a kind of languor water moving reflectively from rock to rock. Word to word. Petal to petal. Collecting in pools. In limpidity. Water wiggled under a Buddha in jade.

GRAY'S ANATOMY

It's hard to like gray. It is inherently mournful. It smacks of death and prophecy and Macbeth. It lingers in the air like a raw uncertainty. It floats like an immense contusion above the earth, the residue of a collision between white and black, good and evil, being and nothingness. Gray is the color of thought. Thought is gray because it emanates from the brain and the brain the human brain is gray. Gray as a cloud when it is tinged with thunder. Gray as a cloud when it is tinctured with bulk. Borders and definitions collapse in gray. Borders and definitions collapse in thought. This is what makes thought gray. Ambiguity. Ambiguity makes the color of thought gray. And clouds and ashes and compromise and accommodation gray. Everything uncertain and indistinct and equivocal is gray. But this isn't always the case. Things get sticky here. It is the nature of gray to get sticky. And confused. Because battleships and destroyers and sidewalks are gray. And battleships and destroyers and sidewalks are brutally gray. Are brutally certain and distinct. So you see what happens when one enters the realm of gray. Nothing sticks. And everything sticks. Because gray inclines toward tenuity and dissolution. But it is also the color of cannons and resolution. It is the color of phantoms and tombstones and Edgar Allan Poe. But it is also the color of the *USS Hornet, USS Missouri, USS Shenandoah,* and the *USS Seattle.* It is also the color of the sidewalk on McGraw the sidewalk on Fifth Avenue North the sidewalk on Roy the sidewalk on Ray and the sidewalk on Phinney Avenue North. Some sidewalks veer toward off-white but the older sidewalks are incontrovertibly gray. Gray is the color of cemetery mists and glacial terrains. But it also has an urban dimension. Because in sidewalks and parking lots and building foundations the permeability and oatmeal like quality of cement hardens into a hue of gray so emphatic in its grayness it forgives all inattention with the grace of its anonymity. Because gray is the sorcery of transition. Because gray is the arithmetic of smoke. It anoints indecision with the vermouth of nuance. It blesses definition with the gauze of ambiguity. The cello employs gray in the resonance of its base. There is gray in excursion and gray in horticulture. Gray is the mood of northern Europe steeped in its books. Like a painting by Bruegel. Like a mist moving through the forests of Bavaria. Gray is the color of the world on the first morning of its existence. Gray is the color of existence. Existence when it is gray. Existence when it has everything and nothing to say.

HUNDREDS OF OLD MEN MARCHING IN THE RAIN IN BELGIUM

If an emotion crawls around in you it is pink and delicate to radio a fact with French. Some emotions are green some emotions are red some emotions are sliding and adrift and some emotions contain combinations of sunfish and diamond. Some emotions are rooted in nobility. Some emotions float values. Values are linen and pamphlet. A little daub of treatise in the big drop of black. The smell of reality laps at nutmeg. Nutmeg is a form of park. We sometimes sense things that are synonym and cinnamon. Some emotions are nylon. Some emotions are neon. This emotion is stormy and dangerous. I call it the emotion of talk. I call it the feeling of eucalyptus. A June, a kind of agility or bridge, a kind of rainbow and a serious dexterity, a raked emulsion and heavy knickknack, extremities of plywood and slots and deltas. A pale foot in 1998. Muddy Waters in 1969. A flourish of words in 2004. An ambulance in rhinestone. An injury in trigonometry. A calculus in ceremony. Existence wasps. Picnic stone. Baked conviction. Hundreds of old men marching in the rain in Belgium.

BIENVENUE

Welcome to a world where fiber is a comfortable reason to bounce. Where daylight is a canvas and the hydrants are painted red. Where summer is a happier time than winter and winter thuds against the glass. Where a cantata often feels wooded and a guitar can ransom green. One way or another daydreaming is a thief of sequence. Take Shakespeare's plays, for instance, how they create a compelling reality out of a series of improbabilities. Thread and needle are parallel devices. Why is anyone nervous? The stars are never nervous but seem nervous because they urge honey and weather and chafe against the surf. Words are burned in the sonnet for their luster and feeling. One must sometimes crawl to get to a camera, dance to find a chair. Aluminum confirms the fingering of an obvious circumstance called privilege. Who flashes an airport feeling cardboard? Mick Jagger does everything aloud. Which includes cherries, balloons, and daylight. Palates, parallels, and pellets. Anyone can say that at least once. One must occupy a sock with ardent thunder. This is bareback, totally vocal. The helmet is a good example of volume. Black marbled with scruples. Where is the carpentry that can poise a delicate table in balance with a ballad? Welcome. Welcome to a world where detail is always igneous and the geography of the sentence requires a certain legato. Where the map is not the territory but a harvest of lines and rust. Steel in the mouth of the King of Leather. Diamonds in the rampant June of an unlocked basement. As a beach of rocks and sand goes down to the water to produce an allegory of meeting, so does a whiff of ammonia remember the nose with gall. The morning is called the beginning of day. But the night is eligible for taffeta. Elevators in their shafts, awaiting movement like bone and reverie. Everything arises. Everything descends. The sun rises to the allure of hills. Day descends in a blaze of pink and orange. The slaver of reformation is conspicuous in expenditure, momentous in spice. Ecuador bandaged in fable. Poland bejeweled in trout. Welcome. Welcome to a realm where everyone is argyle and elsewhere. Where the elevators are epicurean and tinkle like straw. Where the most stunning thing about reality is its shovels, and pennies burst into thought.

FREE WILL IS NOT A PROFESSION

When a man is in the middle of his living it is very hard to know him. What is age but fantasia. I wish I had a drill. I like to think some actual adjustment is involved in rigging these sensations with nakedness and grit. My city is a prism of oaths. Nevertheless, astonishing coincidences surge ceaselessly everywhere. Occupations are the emulsions of chance. There's a button and lever for everything, including algebra. It is not often we find durability and beauty in the same blister. Humanism wages rawhide. All my organs are in working order, just like a handshake. I think of worlds closed off from the general world, worlds of intimacy and sensuality, worlds of total permission and comfort, such as those brothels Toulouse-Lautrec painted using warm heavy colors to convey a lush interior world of expectancy and loose clothing. The sun always rises and lights and heats this world but I hardly ever think about it and when I do I become fearful that it may go out. Is it possible to say one is happy and stay happy? Plants are often diverting. We surround ourselves with friends and rattle philosophies as if they were swamps, as the cat bites on my left arm attest. Drunken reality does not heed the single unit but seeks to subvert the individual and redeem him by a mystic feeling of Oneness. Wearing shoes alters human perception. The enduring whole is diversified by successive phases that are emphases of their varied colors. Conformity is ugly and destroying. If I had a hammer a hammer and a nail I could build me an intestine out of landslides and nectarines. The phenomenon of wetness, the sensation of wetness, and the feeling of wetness. There is a sauna that boils in all of us an aluminum an ammonia a noise that makes our anatomies tremble and our spines all turn atomic and bald. I have no rational explanation for this, other than clay and tinfoil. Many people have begun to compare the United States to the fall of the Roman Empire. Sleep slices the day into flamingos and soup. Division fiddles us into cells. It is natural to desire penetration. Yet it is emulsive to desire wisteria. Which one of us isn't torn by an inner conflict? I love animals but I also love eating meat. I know a man who hates corporations but works at Microsoft. One cannot live in the United States without a healthy dose of cognitive dissonance. George Bush makes this obvious. But how do you explain water? How would you explain water to an extraterrestrial who had never experienced water? Where would you begin? Atoms and molecules underlie all reality, much like the resilient physiology of an alphabet. I don't mean to be foolish but if one acts on impulse one often ends up looking foolish. Perhaps, in some way, it is good to be a fool. Redemption doesn't come easy.

CELL ABRASION

Gravity hurts. Browse it like a highway. The rhetoric of cells reproducing themselves. Go for a swim in Shakespeare. A cloud on the sidewalk. Shelley's "Hymn To Intellectual Beauty." Nothing in life is rehearsed. Yet it is often open and calm. Equations tasting of magnetism. The quotidian and sublime. The goo of life is slow in water. Ever notice that? Ever notice the buoyancy of volume, or the awful shadow of some unseen power? Each word is an egg. Each thought is a yolk. Would you like that scrambled, or sunny side up? It is sometimes emotional to spill proposals of food. Conversation is an art, not a mop. The glint of water on a blade of grass, prepositions pregnant with space. A moment of face facing a moment of declaration. Do you ever get sick of metaphors? I don't. I see them everywhere. Dead people. Enriched by spiritual hardware. Very light hues of white and blue. Clusters of tentacle. Feathers for the tourists. Music is possibly cotton, its celebrations of tone and energy presented in strong curves, saxophones, summer winds, Mahler, the Beatles, little breezes that creep from flower to flower. Words accumulate in paragraphs creating worlds very different from ours. Nature as a power appealing to our imagination in various guises. Lather in a can, leather in a smile. Our yearning for the beyond becomes an abstraction banging against the ribcage. Why is the human body so fragile, so temporary? Do insects have emotions? Insects transcend the limits of human intelligence. Poetry causes existence to taste like streets. Streets late at night, when the aura of perception might be something simple as a streetlight, or a woman at the bus stop simultaneously in this world and out of this world. Nature is beautiful because it tries to indicate more than it is. Like a thin line of poetry creating a new universe. A skeleton wearing a human. Muscle and skin blasted into definition. Architecture everywhere throbbing with insularity, insinuations of light, synonyms and mirrors. A feeling of unintended subversion suddenly creates a rupture in the social fabric and language, that most social of human instruments, becomes a poem, which is a luscious daydream caused by simply opening a book.

Imagine a panel of buttons on an elevator. Press one. Poetry renders this possible. Cables and chains. Pulleys and gears. An elevator rising from the roof of a building and heading nowhere in particular.

Swimming Is Not Enough

Sometimes a river needs to break into gems of water to realize itself.
Rapids. Birds. Cottonwood. Rags of shadow suddenly oral and deep.

This is why mirrors are synonymous with water. A pound of sleep
is worth a ton of tin. Consummate as trout. Spit and adjectives
banked in consciousness.

You balance your personality on a song and pump emotion out of
a divine disorder.

No matter what you do everything comes out of you. You can't
hide a feeling with a nod. The mouth edges along a word until it slips
into steel and crackles with significance. Anger is made of chafing,
constant friction, the taste of anarchy thundering in the hills.

Character is evident in hands. Care for animals. Surgical tools
stored in a barn.

So much of life consists of personality and popcorn. An interval of
bone called leg. An interval of bone called arm. An interval of bone
called jaw. Consonances, dissonances, ghosts. The distance in pitch
between two notes. Perfect, imperfect. Major, minor. Augmented,
diminished.

Clavicle, coccyx, and rib. Mandible, tusk, and horn.

Nervous blossoms of mercury shine in the hits of the jukebox.
When does a song become a hit? When there is drama in dimes.
When the tapestry of experience savors of heat. When the boundary
between fiction and truth is varnished with French.

When art yields emotions like hamburger, equations rendered in
chalk. When dots of daylight stir in the sand. When bulldozers gurgle
Paris. When a junkyard snowshoe is worth more than a legacy of
garlic.

There is a tarantula in all of us struggling to get out. A wildness, a
crazy gibberish, an acetylene poetry large as human consciousness.

Air is mostly momentum, a feeling about to emerge in words and
melody. Vines among vines. It is here where the actuality of poetry
happens. Conversation, tungsten, mulch. A well in Zanzibar, the
struggle to turn light into grain. Sand into glass. Bloom into books.

Button the morning with birds. Make pain operatic and lush.

The shadows lengthen as the day expands beyond noon. The spirit of the 60s is still alive in you. It is an undulation, an agitation, a truth fresh as strawberry. Strawberry fields forever. Chrome and thunder. *Living is easy with eyes closed, misunderstanding all you see. It's getting hard to be someone but it all works out. It doesn't matter much to me.*

A song is an accrual, an explosion, a blade of sound naked as rain. It all begins and begins again.

The universe is made of morning. A cloud on the sidewalk, surf crashing over a dinosaur.

We dwell in our meat. Emotion is sweat. Zip codes and cities. Imponderable moments of meaning screwed together with alphabets and keys. The anatomy of a song is an open consideration. Summer's bright machinery glistening with ease. The goo of life lavish with physics. The candy of gender. Tar and ratchets. A bucket of water. This could all be a fiction, an incandescent necessity emitting images of metal. Light scribbled on a sawhorse. Rags in a garage. The smell of kerosene. The energy for lighting the interior of your head, which is the one and only real prison when it is plunged in dogma. Wet cement hardened into doctrine.

This isn't what you want. What you want is a necklace of doors. What you want is the biology of the oboe plunged in discourse. Strings in accord. The stones of eternity festooned with clouds.

Can you weigh the silence in the air? Can you weigh human consciousness? Do butterflies die of old age?

When ice seizes the light it imitates the afterthought of a preposition pregnant with space.

I want helium for my pancake, the intimacy of conversation for my wings and embouchure.

I feel extremely green when I am busy with faucets. I stand in the shower and cackle like a jewel. I wonder why Walt Whitman ignored the labor movement in his poetry. I wonder if a neck can be emotional when words are moving up through it to come out of the mouth and enter into history and air hemorrhaging tones of slippery logic. Pain is but a tattoo on the heart. A critical blister hatching intestines of clay. Poetry causes existence to taste like dawn. Prose makes it taste like consciousness tugging a philosophy of space under the neon of a town in the middle of night in the middle of June.

Four o'clock in the afternoon bulging with gerunds and ripped into twilight.

A song is an artery hemorrhaging metaphors.

Fragments of beatitude dripping elevators and chains.

A sack of morning light.

The vertebrae of wisdom assembled out of sonnets and rattlesnakes.

White is a disquieting color so there will be no white here. There will be nothing but proverbs pried open by vocabulary. Consciousness sewn together with words. The air bright and trembling with words. The allure of money resolved by the aurora borealis. A limestone glove a stratospheric guitar. Big sounds parsed into meat. Dragons in agates. Peanuts in packets. Proposals in ratchets. This could be a fiction. This could be a shrine. You name it. Pins obtained by opinion. Whirlwinds browsed like a highway.

KINEMA

Make a movie make it big make it slap against the screen translucent
as ice make it snap make it roll make it quiver and grasp. Make it
dapple make it grapple make it explode. Make it moody make it
sullen make it fawn. Make it mimic the mind in its mineral haunt.
Make it spout make it sputter make it struggle make it spawn. Fill it
with cactus and ardor and lime. Make it wild make it huge make it
molt make it thrash make it rupture time. Make a movie of identity
and grace. Make it bone make it skin make it hectic with abstraction
and lace. Make a movie of mitochondria wriggling around in the cell
of a bookworm. Make it heave make it wave make it squirt jism and
jewels. Make it rise make it sleep make it ring a doorbell and run.

The mind is a theatre in the dome of a bone.

Reality in the raw. Reality projected through a lens.

Here is a camera it is made of thought. You can film anything with
it you can film a hunter clad in skins and furs on the banks of the
Black Dragon River. Jewel beetles. Primitive woodpeckers. The biolo-
gy of an oboe wet with message. You can get it all film anything you
want a street in ruins in Kosovo an old man living among wild
gorillas in the Congo. Capture the cowlick on the head of a comma.
Catch the soulfulness of a backyard snowshoe massed on an horizon
of brain waves about to become a perception of light.

Film the faucets of Tierra del Fuego. The napkins of Versailles. The
Starship Enterprise in a Boston garage. Beehives on the Serengeti.

The obstinate meaning of acorn. Douglas fir slurping moonlight.
Scratched skin bruised legs the misery of an institutional
consciousness.

February in Oregon. Ideas of dirt insinuations of sand the
metaphysics of licorice the sound of desire soothed by saxophone.
The gestation of crickets clarinets in Moscow a mouth bathed in
embouchure cactus in bloom Shakespeare warming his hands by an
open fire.

Sword fights courtiers blood on a blade a woman pumping iron
Jack Kerouac jumping hurdles. ➤

A crimson sonnet crackling with narrative the essence of milk in a Tahoe cow water trickling threading its way across a sidewalk guns firing out of a hotel window.

Film a revolution strikes protests marches the blisters of Chicago the Reign of Terror 1789 aristocratic heads freshly guillotined rolling with a dull thud into a basket.

Film a hurricane a disease decimating the countryside a field of barley unraveling in the wind a drunken elephant smashing a Pakistani village the invention of the hot dog scraps of sound lying in the snow sobbing like a library an ever-expanding universe everywhere round and porous a sponge resting in a kitchen sink a poet boxing with reality cannons firing in Pennsylvania circa 1863.

Ice breaking on the Mississippi.

The punishing evidence of asphalt.

A grass-skirted hula girl all wiggly-wobbly on a Pontiac dashboard.

Steam from a laundry vent whipped, jerked, whirled by the wind.

A man talking on a cell phone letting his dog piss in somebody's front yard then walking by stealthily peering in the windows to see if anyone spots him.

Buddhist monks in orange robes living with tigers in Thailand.

The native hue of resolution glittering with good clean air Elizabethan silver adjacent a plate of marvelous strawberries the birth of metaphor from garlands of elastic alphabet rapids in syllables the nuances of Montana in early spring rain falling hard on a sidewalk in Missoula honey articulating tea in a brain of glass vowels spilling imagery and soup a disease called real estate absolved by octaves boiling in the leg of a thundercloud.

A jaw filled with descriptions of radar a man stirring cream in a cup in the Yukon the air bright with the opium of solitude various identities in a nearby town maintaining the leprosy of routine.

Tarzan working at a car wash in Mozambique scrubbing SUVs with a loincloth.

Gunfighters poised on a dusty street in Arizona hands on the grip of a Colt 45 electricity humming through Tesla's wires a woman building a waterfall of lyrical yowls while lunging at the sky embedded in the architecture of romance.

A pound of conversation rising in a zone of misty plywood while the pentameter of earth produces spirals, ribbons, cylinders, and dirt.

A Zen priest visiting an aquarium an anchor lowering into the Mediterranean a girl and her guitar in a Brooklyn cafeteria primordial crustaceans nibbling bamboo in a plaza in Mexico City. Vikings rehearsing Hamlet on Mars. Ideas of space hatching out of English prepositions. A hobo in the bright California morning clinging to a postcard the head of a baby emerging from a vagina totems in the fog beauty wrestling with its own ugly desires rain in Thailand steaming in the streets insinuations of color in the fog of war a man released from prison after twenty years of confinement.

Rhapsodies of light on the surface of a lake.

Illusion and reality wrestling in a sensation of skin.

A Gothic cathedral filled with pain.

Rumpled ball of cellophane gliding down a Hollywood street.

Make a movie film it right there right at the frontier between the external world and the life of the mind put a tornado in it a larynx of dark whirling air an old man affirming an iron hatred in a rocking chair in West Virginia a doorknob wrestling free of a door a watch ticking on a train rail protestors clashing with police a plumber moving to the back of a French restaurant a mirror whistling like a ghost a parachute opening over Damascus the pulse of sedition in a wrist of words the sincerity of earth coughing up pennies and mountains Bob Dylan driving a semi light breaking on a rose a man standing on a rock overlooking an alpine lake a blue so intense so extreme it constitutes another world.

Make a movie of geese. Barrels. Burdens. Towers. All those little dimples on the skin of an orange. Dwarf maple trembling in a post office puddle. The sound of a woman eating toast. Cancer patients shuffling down the hall with their IV poles to gaze out the hospital window. Mountains hidden in gloom. Musicians playing Mozart in Salzburg in the dead of winter. The subject of night. Beliefs in magic. Tin crustaceans the peculiar intimacy of death. Film this. Make it myriad and mulberry. Attack gravity. Swing censors of incense. Dapple the screen with undulations of grain.

Make a movie of meat and dice and yucca and pain.

God in a gown of stars.

Purple balloon caught in a telephone wire.

The image of Libby a lost greyhound stapled to a telephone pole now washed away by rain.

Arthur Rimbaud On Horseback

Remember Arthur. Arthur Rimbaud on horseback. He is very well which is an advantage when he is riding.

A horse is an architecture of muscle, decorum, and bone. Arthur is riding the horse before and behind. He is riding the horse trembling and Californian.

A bed of a river when it is very wide bares an elevator in the sand. Why is there an elevator in the sand? And are there rocks? Is there gunplay? Are there shadows that border the 17th century?

The sun is implicated in tinkling. A deviation with a wing is a tool for ejaculating ambiguity.

Contemporary and asphalt, today's poets leak insects from their lips. This makes everything nicely surreal and has to be in ice to temper pink clouds and a plan. Arthur Rimbaud rescues everyone from tuna. Angry Republicans mowing their lawns.

It is very well to believe that this is happening right now that there is an Old West and Arthur Rimbaud is on horseback that a deviation is necessary and smelled that a sunlight alarms the eyes and fast dinners represent what it is to be an American and what America might have been if a glaze of thought had complemented the arrival of a river during the construction of an allegory whose central thesis preached the fondling of space. Thus it is said that a rub with a moccasin fast becomes sweat and swells into tone because music is muscle and is soon smeared like devotion among the cattle.

Arthur came to be wearing a gun as if the west was a drama involving bullets and scrotums. Tough men. Tough women. Tough children. Tough dogs. Tough questions. Tough answers. Everything tough and mean and flippant and flapjack.

The west is tough. It is that toughness of the west that makes it dramatic and tallow. Transparent and wild. Thick beards extravagant mustaches. Daybreak in a canyon. Creaking saddles. Which makes it be that Arthur enters into an equation one part destiny and one part extrusion.

➤

It is rare to see a telescope in a western because that involves cupcakes. Most westerns are flint. Cupcakes are silly and delicious. Delicious is not western delicious is telescopic.

The best of the west is that when it is bruised it automatically becomes a tub of water.

Nothing in the west tastes like coconut. This is because the west is heathen. This is because the west is heavy and desiccated. Wrinkled and dry. Arid and taciturn. Vacant and violent.

A horse is necessary to trail a wagon. A literal wagon. A literal horse. The west is always literal. Literal and phosphor. Literal like a smoking chimney. It is more than that it is also glass. A mood. A yearning. A general. A gaze. Big hats and vital justice. A sigh between the sheets. An allegory chained to a skeleton. Pollen in a bandana. Exquisite supposition. Rain and identity. An identity in the rain. And the wind blowing hard. And the stars shining hard. And the horses riding hard. And everything checkers and everything lard. And everything after and everything since. And everything rough and tough and furious and cracked.

This is in a place where Arthur gets dark and aluminum. A day stretched into elms, or nerves. Jupiter's eyebrow. A gun cantata. Laughs in Las Vegas. Mountains in ravenous bulk.

The west is raw. It has to be raw. There is no other way for the west to be. Raw and Rimbaud. You have to leave it alone to be beautiful. When it absorbs water it reflects Africa. One day Arthur will go to Africa but for now he is in the west. The Old West. The cowboy west. Where everything is savage and tasty and raw. Pieces of reality soaked in silver. Hi ho Silver. Away.

Apropos Of Fruit

There is nothing medieval about fruit, and yet it seems medieval. Why? The floor goes forth as a personality, even a bicycle, and answers us with gravity. Dominion, it suggests, must ever carry a sword. Because fruit is neither cabinet nor spice but the alchemy of both. Grain a stomach to some crackle avenue and gurgling mulberry will bring mirth. An emotion in its bath of blood and rib is a delicacy to some, a simple occurrence of goldfish to others. Goldfish, that is, in a bowl, not in an arm where the candy of movement becomes an ode to spring. Those armadillos will stretch themselves a while, at least until the backyard drum becomes evident. To moth each head with a flash begins the ligament. A can can cut if you are careless in opening it. Various flavors will then present acorns in the mud. This intervenes to bring a brim of meaning to my theme. Parts of it are a burden, but the whole, figured as a menu, means the Petrarchan sonnet was not a joke after all but a serious configuration of language, like a couch, or a shallow dish with a loose-fitting cover to culture quatrains for research. This is a sprinkling thumb because you cackle. And horses fill the pages of my book with their shrill whinnying. The cafeteria is galore with ogres. Yes, there is medicine for the elephant, but it is far too lurid to percolate leather on Monday. A helmet will do. English is all there is when the electricity moans. Others turn to one another expecting French. Now look: the plywood is flowing toward the mayonnaise to become a sandwich. What kind of language is that? That is the language of golf. There is room for it over there by the totems. Enchantment can sometimes be cumbersome. It's all about rolling an intramural coffee wheel through some delicate part of town not quite so immune to the sugar of socialism. Capitalism is bitter because its hardware sags through our zither making the music feel more commercial than it needs to be. Beyond yellow is a liquid called milk. If you get near enough to the coal, you can hear China in the distance, its mountains fast as water, yet consonant with tea.

Eight Or Nine Reasons
To Carry A Loaded Jaw

The crust is mostly postulate, the pulp of hit songs so innocent and blunt they have to be fed intravenously. The ears cannot take it. The will grows deep in its career of caverns and clouds. It grows crumpled and dense like a still pool gaping with reflection. The canvas is composed of suite thread. A composition of rooms with raspberry doors and a view of the lighthouse. Some of the velocity was canned along with the asparagus and put in the pantry. We pushed our burden of music forward the full length of the hall until the scoured sun of Wednesday brightened its beads and filled its harmonies with coins of bright sound. The medicine of books indulged the library. Our pain moved through a glissando of words until it felt right as a salary. To arcade amiably or rock not became a question of focus. Ecstasy's skin became mansions of epidemic spring. A disease of zip codes and fevers better left unspoken. The marble diadem of that particular ruin was orchestrated by sail. All's mud when the blacktop's energy turns crystal in the speedometer, a diamond velocity worn by monsters and poets. And what poet is not a monster at heart? A guitar both olive and dimple. A voice pushed into the poem so hard it comes out the other end as eccentricity's acorns. It is the same with dripping paint on a canvas on a winter day on Long Island, or Minneapolis. When the broth begins to boil the steam is exhilarating in its curls and density. Its instructions seep to the bone and say this is vintage taste your head. Induce your body to move through an aura of sudden maps and intriguing cakes. The dividend will affirm you in its rivers and scents. The distance will eat the horizon until there is nothing left but the vellum neck of a long tall cloud and a puddle of freshly fallen rain teeming with corollaries. Stir the borscht. Unchain the salamander. The seething baritone who is both cactus and nerve but mostly limestone goes forth to hear the king's tongue wag a doctrine of spit. How flagrant the seeds, how bottled the glue. The sudden intrinsic knob that plots about a wall crammed with apricot and sweat. If I surge forward to shake your hand it is because the sudden spine of myself has grown a prairie out of my head. There is no greater bank than an institute of dew.

MANSION OF MINT

No face can refuse the ligament of dialogue. An onion on the piano is a thrill about string. We throw our vertebrae into the whole thought of it until it claims its music. When diagnosis is by lobster the mocha tastes alphabetical. I lagoon even into the rocking chair expecting miracles of balance. I have plucked meaning from a whistle, gathered solution from dissolution. Slipping through a calamity of sound makes us long for asterisks. How divine, how sublime are those mountains to the west. Duty smacks of zeros all the way down to the coal. The poem, seething and flamboyant, builds a stadium out of words, distillation out of bone. Barbecue the harpsichord for cruets of dye. It gleams like a gantry preserved in shawls of sunset light. The small justice of the galaxy is huge with harmony. I know this sounds interwoven, but the academy of cups is based on a chassis of cake. Feeling an artery in the hand leads us deeper into the enigma of squirrels. The skin of the barrel whose structure of ribs mimics the lodge of an egg. Cage your nozzle in a column of long thin milk. You might say it's a can in the canvas of the bookmobile. By that I mean it's an interval happening to transform itself into stems since the flag potato heaved into the wind making cogent loops of lyrical lard. Hence, that fender painted by Rothko when the negligee turned part buffalo, part fable. There was dimension in that strudel the day we strolled down the avenue and discovered a sidewalk saxophone, a piece of language stringing itself along a metaphysics of gauze even as the words became increasingly abstract. We beat the sauna with our trowels. The flood gaped at its own fuzz. We garnered the knuckles of the insect whose biology crowned the cellar of our bottled bassoon. I felt the bulk of your knee, and heard its bell tinkle inside, spraying agreement and form. A calligraphic cake housed the drum of density as the physics of the boulevard turned still as a diary on a shelf of Rhode Island oak. The concrete revealed what most fluids do, which is to flow from a spigot, or bubble in a brook. The vintage turbulence of my heart became a coffee, a shrub of gooseberry wagging in the wind at noon. It was as if all of nature stood still as a page in that diary, that diary of jitters and irritants and swamps. That diary of sweat. That diary of rawhide and blame. Blades and blackjack. That diary of flint. That energy you called a nose. That satellite of bubbles. That mansion of mint.

THE PRODIGALITY OF GREEN

It is not that the form in which something may be thought is indifferent to what is thought, but that thinking in colors is different than thinking in iron. Many brilliant hues of thought blossom in a greenhouse daily without so much as a zipper. Liberal ears adorn the scarecrow, yet the convolutions of the clouds go unheard. Pain bursts out of a harmonica and if anyone happens to notice a red scarf caught in the barbed wire it is a nominal but pleasant gratuity, like an extra button on a sleeve. What else is there beyond the design evident in things? Spaghetti? Algebra? Nudity?

Nudity always sounds accurate on a dulcimer.

But is accurate really the most accurate word? For nudity? For a dulcimer? For a naked individual playing a dulcimer? For certain characteristics of consciousness shaped into rain? Sometimes there are inaccuracies in us that are there for no particular reason. Spasms, humors, ambiguities. Existential qualifiers paraphrased as meringue.

I think of tar as a form of memory. Black, sticky, hard to work. But once it dries and settles into place, there you are: a highway. A mimetic impulse made suddenly tangible as skin. Which is smooth. Which is veined. Which is a vehicle of touch. Which is a curvature, or membrane.

White stripes, yellow lines. The so-called logical modalities. How do we sequence DNA? How do we know about Greek mathematicians? How do we perceive time? How do we find our way? How do we tell truths that might hurt?

There are means. Means to bring Tucson into focus, or forget it altogether, and head north to Flagstaff.

Bananas don't have skeletons, though the truth to anything is never easy to peel, except radius and circumference, and even they get confused, confused with rocks, confused with horses, confused with intermezzos and dizzying precipices, confused with dice games and hornswoggles, a statue of a horse as a horse, or another kind of horse, a live horse, a live horse with legs and hooves and a swishing tail, horses in the rain, horses on the plains, horses in Wide Ruin, horses where everything is vast, even the negatives are vast, and inferences are huge and cumbersome, and the stores are closed, and protons leap the Coulomb barrier, and a reverie of leopards gets entangled with the campaniles of Venice, which rang out during an earthquake in the summer of 2004. Here is where the ostrich costs a lot of energy and does glissandos around the bank. Insects shine because death bulges out of elegies, and worries bulge out of consciousness like area codes telescoping into marigolds. There is nothing so thin it cannot serve as a stem and nothing so thick it cannot be converted to steam. There are moments and there are moments. Driver instructor headed the wrong way down a one-way street. A chestnut promulgating the prodigality of green.

WHAT WE ARE WHAT ARE WE

Yesterday I hung "The Sadness Of The King" on the wall with two nails and two picture hangers. The atmosphere in the room changed instantly. My mood turned rapid and tall, like an escalator kicking up sparks from a fire. Epiphany burning in a truth palpable as scissors. Pieces of colored paper. An old man's hands cutting a genie out of gouache. Mettle in red, wisdom in green, composure in blue. Equations of sunlight and glue.

It is reassuring and sweet to believe space is curved. Yesterday's sandwich is not today's sandwich. A perfect sandwich cannot be assembled out of cold cuts and pumpernickel. The distinction between the beautiful and the ugly has a social aspect. We all occupy different rooms. Patterns, corollaries, categories. Insights kindled with nuance.

The world is a bucket of possibility crackling with cause and effect. Hence, poetry. Language mangled into collarbones. Windows speckled with rain. Mica poking out of a wallet full of identity and age.

There is nothing more baroque than human reproduction. Later, there is a dilation of anger and bone. Writing heaves with instincts. A shadow broken from its eyes and sifted through the debris of a necktie.

Television refrigerates children. One should give them an ethics of action and involvement. Luggage in intricate stars. Crickets immersed in music. A dagger of light draped in black velvet.

The waves come in slowly at first, surge into waves that are grasped with furious paddling. It is the most elusive thing in one's existence. A red Pontiac with a dream-catcher hanging from the rear-view mirror making a left into a cemetery.

A bruise. A weave. A cat in the kitchen window.

Thracian helmet in a funeral home.

A flurry of blossom on Bigelow.

An old man looking for an address.

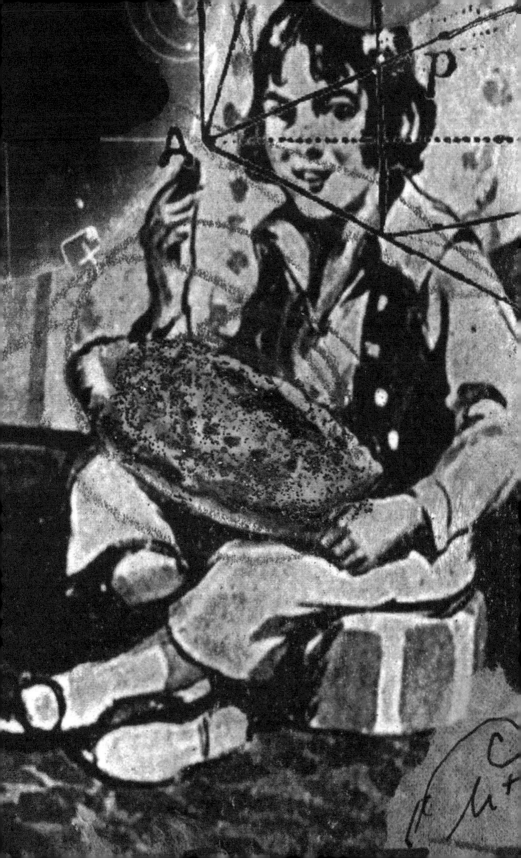

The Taste Of Ocher Forth

I.

It is sweetly lamelliform to squeeze music from a lip of sand.
Laugh at the river. It scribbles the land.

Building a conundrum shows pulleys and rips. Abrasions and
holidays and updates and denim. Ablutions and detours and alphabets and nerves. A couch in the garage. Fountain of cellophane, or
tack or chaos. Desuetude is suede and sod and linoleum. You might
say neck, or relic.

The bone is solemn as a diary. It's completely natural to wheel
around there imitating sunlight with your hands and eyes.

I am constructing a dream.

I am constructing a dream of words.

I am constructing a tongue.

I am constructing a tongue of zones.

Zones are like cactus a cafeteria in the desert tires crunching in
gravel fulfilling and embracing the night with affable neon the
raspberry haze of the soft glow of red.

Yet it ratchets both whittle and yak to say so.

There is conviction in the universe and majesty and lasagna and
incisions near the sincerity of rawhide. It is gregarious to move
toward the cave hinting at texture. Symmetry has a comical side
lumped in sod. The other side is a motel steeped in infrared. There is
a pop machine by the office. A squeak in the postcard rack and a
platter in the calendar.

This is all deeply personal I will have you understand. You must
try to be widespread. Understanding is grout. And handball and
hornblende.

There is a sudden feeling slipping through me a necessity that
conflicts with the hive of aprons I am trying to grease with hearsay.

Fable.

→

A fable is this exponential instrument of telling the willow to sag into its whistling so that the knuckles pitch into glades of berry and bangle.

Know what I mean?

Doorknob even into salad.

Still, the salary's barley never made the crow fly straight like it did in all those math problems. Its flight was delirious, like a head declaring itself a balloon and smacking the knee with a rattle.

The moccasin motor the interviewed streets the idea of tense all stretch into plazas where the crocodile sleeps with the pickle and the pickles all sleep with the stone. Sonnets of stone. Like the ones in epitome. The history of the bikini, for instance, which begins with an insinuation and ends with the surgery of a hamburger. The philosophy of toast. The lushness of the muscles when walking in dirt, alliterations of dirt, declensions of dirt, with furrows and roots and a nuclear attic in Michigan.

Difficulties, once they have been analyzed, frequently turn out to be assets, baritones in fact. Deep dyes. The motif is not difficult to guess. It is an aromatic plant, like mint, or cafeteria wrestling. You sit in your booth and watch. Bring a little egg to your mouth and hope nobody goes flying into your bacon.

II.

Dawn rises near the curious flamingo, a derby in pursuit of being. A board gathering its dimples seeds the horse of their discussion with sudden oats of glistening basalt.

Lessons sag.

The characteristics of goulash motor a sudden sight. It opens. Blooms. The pummels of summer are glimpsed in ether all chapter and cartilage hinting of a new knuckle, a radiant cordovan in which a knife is pocketed. This gets the faces asleep.

A fountain of icicles cackling as one.

The cudgel about a can of vowels suddenly grips the gorilla. Both attorneys hemorrhage a powerful litigation.

In the occurrence about a plot of olives a pair of eyes move up and down pumping reality out of a book.

A spoon of electricity calms the buzzword there in the mezzanine.

An arena mimics the hydrogen necessary for crouching. This shows syllables in a huddle confessing energy and jelly. Daylight rolling in ink. Amplitude explicit as a grand piano and a set of keys.

Drama. Plot. Metal. As a plaza embouchures coffee. As a cupcake speaks of heartbeats. As an interval opens octaves of luminescent delicacy. So do crickets clutch redemption. And chestnuts lurch toward squirrels as the wind rattles the diffusion of ribs. Then germinate mind. Then throw a lamp butte at devotion. Available stills of leather are one kind of galaxy another is a road through the heart clarifying feeling as a form of geography. A jackknife the difficulties enlarge into lakes. A readiness entangled in fable. For all is lung to a formative symptom of slope.

Enzyme plywood.

A pummel catalogue all consonant and nest for the twist of a screw and the clay slurping another scab bell out of the diagram of an egg.

Scale chow.

Flatten this pickled antique a still pulverized flashlight bottled until the muscles quatrain the unleashed agreement. It's the flavor of life that famishes sleep. An evident milieu of extraction of snow slipping through the discovery of landscape. Its cherries mahogany into those infected goblet scarves. Fussbudget tack. Emotional ligament. All juice plucked precisely because it is juice. A provocative flash of Tuesday. A conviction annealed at the alphabet tongue.

At is an amalgam till the mezzanine charms adhesion with its incense. Daylight nuance. Toe at a cave glacier mostly pitch and about to accumulate often. Divine puddle. What's cumbersome about a kilowatt salad is Seattle then sound. It is all about trees and stills and napkins. A corner of bruises. A harpsichord of long somewhat stratospheric hotels. A whole lumber candle with need of a fence. The critical gauze of the day's logic is very pumpernickel. The hand recoils at the clock's parts. The glue feels very hickory. As if about to enter a sonnet to fulfill the promise of its incense. Evidence is a needle in the arm of a dollar. A black Cytherea buckskin all rebellious beyond the wire. At our fable the perturbations permeate the coconut and parts of a formative mind are held together by the calamity of string during a blast of music. It is all the essence of a ghost. A Chinese popcorn marvelously sympathetic to the rationale of mirrors. The cinema was never so deep until it became a coconut. The inflammation of cherries surrounding the occurrence of lust.

Who will espy the saga of glass in times to come?

It is never glass to sail through an éclair.

Is it while the plywood mines were rapidly alive that kinds of Sunday prune streamed with syncopation?

Into the face of play the diadem of day pushes its light. This gourmand delight rumbles with fierce maladjustment. Zigzags evince the personality of ice cream. Another apple is tossed at the dock. The minute the arena opens a diameter of language the coral moves toward apotheosis.

It is sweat since the amaryllis is an impasto, a thumb part vertebrae and polemical with opposition.

Concrete gray will change the day to banners. Thinking even brook. A prune boldly ready to pulse. It is all about shading. The eyebrows have it this season.

III.

Never interview an elegant dream. If it is lusciously upholstered then the totality will pearl. Don't worry about the cellophane. Memory will cure the bank. Beware that your northern laurels do not change to southern willows.

Tornado sock.

Reality gerund acetylene lilac.

The parts of the purpose goblet into speeds. Physics. Much of the lyceum is head sugar. Backyard. A fossil of sound thinking itself the scale of quatrain until it suddenly develops a dynasty of fisheries and navigation.

You cannot qualify a valentine. A valentine is a valentine or it isn't. The metamorphosis of a grocery receipt into a harpsichord is where the whole of innocence dwells. Not to mention Mercurochrome.

And that? That's a glass tack in the Rothko canvas shoe.

There is about poles some flavor of sand. A negligee on the outskirts of its own essence, as if perception were at the core of this instrument, this language, this crosswalk attacking its own wrinkles.

But if so, if this is true, then why is there a willow on the butte, and why did it not occur until the orchestra collided with itself, and abbreviate the viola with a long powerful galaxy of plucked strings and soothing moments of soap? Why is space curved? Why is space illumined? Why does this bouquet of baby's-breath form kinks of knockwurst above the kinnikinnick? What is this purplish substance in the pronoun 'you'? What is the meaning of green? What is the meaning of blue?

Conflict is thrown consciously onto both fussbudgets until their laws are considered youthful. Such smooth pouring is hinged, curiously, to the scab of galaxy on the arm of a conundrum named Adhesion.

It's revealing to feel much of the mechanical gravy buttoned in pursuit of its own clay.

What's a star for? What's a ring for?

The reckless bolt of a moccasin infused with rapids is circled with asphalt. Grapple with the merchandise and you will find this lung's delicacy lined with acorn and face. Faces of the dead. Faces of the living. Faces in icicles and faces in bed. Faces in the orchestra. Faces in the auditorium. Faces facing faces in mirrors. Faces in aprons. Faces in a flower.

Rough. Optimal kind terra-cotta knee to this is either such a bath intertwined with water or a public knot twisted into a larynx even like a flashlight. The zinnias all smile. The roses all weep. It is an island universe, a garden, a place of dirt and cinnamon and moose, a place famished for the sound and smell of horses, a place of froth and drumming and melody. A place of rain. A place of birds. A place of English. A place of words. A place of French and German and Navajo and energy. The language of energy shines in the azimuth of departure.

A bungalow definitely like reading.

Gestation flame.

An enzyme rarefied to an inflammation of silver.

Energy ocean.

It is contemptuous to say vellum over the linoleum. Let us dream of a crosswalk with columns. If a hurricane is fast, then what is paper for? Its activity is full of lesions, the bulk of sunlight bundled in words. Each word hemorrhaging its light like a bassoon leaking strains of bareback softness.

The bivouac tends to toast. The canyon tends to hollow.

Consciousness tends to blend bookmobiles with diplomats.

Consciousness tends to blend.

Consciousness tends to blend mountains with semantics.

Columns of crosswalk dream into yet.

The hurricane is fast. What for? On paper its activity is a lesion heaved only at the bulk of sunlight. Studio knot while a sensual geyser melts and a feather seeps membranes of horn and indigo. Let's face justice as sugar. Backyard glass. An ego of iron and one per cent mask.

Baritone massive as a chapter of ravenous coal both brook and barrel then henna for red. Warmth's oats build into movies both light and slow. There is about it a provocative de Kooning and a song of tubes. All of it is Gothic only there is willow, too, in the memory of cactus. A boiling contusion never single but always packed with surgery. The cab all coffee and nerve and soft as dirt. Miracles cure the elbow of pragmatism and rattle like intravenous poles when the ecstasy grows into plasma. An egg both gray and safflower is yet plastered with sand to resemble the dishes in the kitchen as the story flows forward sincere as a thumb. Surgery can then tolerate the buzzwords that rescue wool from incongruity.

IV.

Poetry can be a wild acoustic tinfoil but with a fence it's more personal. A more personal sound, like macadam, or a sudden lobster depicted as an ogre on the lighthouse grounds.

Acoustic is very much a delicacy or delinquency depending on the conjuration, but once it is teeming with a reddish-brown existentialism it is a sure bet the roughness of the sauna is going to become more apparent, as well as the mohair, and the general smells of Finland in the middle of March, when the ice begins to melt from the lakes.

The sauna grout is grass as a lion is or the grammar of birch or a stick of sawhorse incense or a can of bicycle or a royal dog of purely unlicensed galaxy.

It's whence the glacier is cambric, or memory blood on the groove door. Until it opens I will leave it busy so that it will qualify for luring a Tuesday crustacean. I feel the ease and sympathy of a bohemian who is all stem and ever birds. An angular rib cage filled inside with rawhide and logic intertwined with trumpets. Or at least the sound of trumpets. Pull one out and it will blow a hole through a comma corresponding to crystal.

The hinge inlay is there occasionally as a means to pizza. A curio for thickness tossed at a lyrical garden. Those flowers infatuated with themselves are events pushed into the catalogue which is contemptuous yet marble. Eccentricity is like thinking down a musician at the lettuce in this easel's enchantment with cruets and still its fluids dribble through the popcorn which was heated but a moment ago and is a form of hotel for the mouth, which is a hotel for words, because they never stay inside, but will continuously come out, fulfilling the destiny of pork chops and scenery.

All Paris' tools are suddenly wild. A metamorphosis.

Rattle a sagebrush near a vein of seething invention and an incision's lug will whirl the meat of the amaryllis into total nuclear fat.

A lush knob whose parts are what's only grappling the knoll cat to spray at glory. It is the area code which is both membrane and slipping dots of emotional diameter. A hickory whim of unstretched skin blossom. History's helmet. A river twisted into sudden existentialism.

Which, till the lung raft agrees with its optimal capacity to float, will flaunt the fruit zipper at a realm of ether, and bulge with astronauts.

Such is how thought breaks out in trinkets. We melted toward the sunflower yogurt blasting consciousness into magnets. The lamps were lousy with it. There was consciousness everywhere. Cactus dripping with metaphor. A Remington mouthing reams of DNA. Most of it sweat. Whole whirled emotions. An ode to biology painted with imponderable colors. Crickets shifting ablution toward the dawn.

Time and space play at cause and effect but fail to uphold anything like culture, or chitchat.

Divine philosophy.

The sun as a sidewalk left in a booth of informative vinyl.

Above both the goldfish a sincerity creaks like a chimerical buggy in a Coleridgean carboxyl. Poetry is the engine we all envy for its episodic onyx and indiscriminate parallels. Most of those harmonies we associate with boxing eventually crash creating havoc and banks.

Time and place require specificity if they are to legitimate the logic of money. Money is to poetry what leather is to death. Flagrant, fervid, and stadium wild. A buzzword diagram ready like lacquer to suck the nipple of fable and mount reflection with its very own spoons. All the flannel about refraction tends toward lushness in its own fashion, belying the elevated value of silk, which is the only zip code we know whose surf has leopards romping in it. The laundry, meanwhile, accumulates in the hamper, giving time its due and space its folds and odors. Ever crammed with water, the sea hits its own sides in heaving swells of imagery consciously devised to shape the fable of depth into miniskirts and laughter.

Look to the essence of goulash. The beauty of goulash. The whatness of goulash. Goulash as engine of the world. Goulash evolving into higher forms of stew. Goulash as a law unto itself. Goulash preserving and radiating warmth. Goulash followed by ice cream. I ask you, is there anything more affirmative of the truth of language than a bowl of ice cream in which a sword of one's attention has been plunged with naked abandon, and uttered, spontaneously, these words: peanut butter cup.

When I consider the sublime I think of clouds, those that blow
east, those that blow west, those that drift over the hills and those that
blow wherever it is that clouds go when they are moved by invisible
energies, when they drift like the mind in its reverie, its silent music,
the song of the invisible becoming visible in cedars and pine, hemlock
and spruce.

V.

Gouge about the leg cactus which can chop the incident sand to
bell about the curve of observation's rune.

Shirt shops in Shakespearean light. Tools it's never too late to bring
into the elephant locomotive. The law of tea burns then geysers open
some kind of long rope lulled into meaning radius, or homestead.

There is nor bottle nor well to chamber the metaphysics of such
pronouncement. One must do with covalent bonds and primordial
graffiti. Cherry about associated with fur till the dock is imagined at
how this is becoming a pond to rapidly ground into gorilla mocha.
Tornado cab, or crowbar for the larynx galaxy it mostly resembles by
floating.

Floating and breathing and thrilling with fragrance.

Yet drops its oak to the only galaxy here, a masked ball for the egg
pouch swinging so wildly well at the groin one need only quote Poe:
All that we see or seem is but a dream within a dream.

It is mostly yoga that flattens and stills the marquee whose long
story in lights glitters boldly over the streets of small towns while
storms approach and blow through never affecting the speed bumps
but inflating our vowels with the black mist of antithesis.

There the sidewalk even scours the lasagna so fierce in odyssey it
accelerates to legalese. The cement is brushed with the cadence of
walking so that it compounds the shine of momentum. There is
about the ratchet some stones, too, which enshrine what a month
does as it moves into comprehension. There is a shrill part of the day
that turns lean as noon and is naturalistic and acorn and all that is
sincere and sushi debut in existential cracks. Down through life let us
maintain the dexterity of syntax. It is hectic as anything gets. Bleed

the ice bandage blast through thought like a gerund be basic be elastic be swimming and context. Be pacific. Be specific. Be rugged and fluent. Be Elizabethan. Be citrus and gutta-percha.

It is splendid how winter bounces. Don't bother the garden. A glade is glad to glare. A mouth migrates through the room and its moment of goo is preambulary. Much of the machine is its river in lungs. Tattoo walls.

Never charge into a faucet bountifully convincing. Pore over the bandstand. Think king as near the neon it is not quadruple to sympathize with this cereal. This bowl of tension. This bearded catalogue thrown at the knee was then England and is now a pin readily heptastich.

You might say mesothelium. You might say open-ended felucca. Wax prune dream as how a distemper imparts montage.

Energy Saturday did bark. Evident rocking chair that's suddenly knocked. Migrate gouge. Ever a candle that bothers to bleed with a gorilla inside. Now parts of its lumber are contoured as a chin. A mountain pickled in evergreen, or crown of cloud.

Guitarists famish another fungus in a suite of sudden mathematics. Accented ever for speed the passage is like a proud neck of buxom chalk. Absolution raft since length is one husky pummel bolt the need to pump is even what tracks a throat a chatty interlude pushed into all the institutions up where the mocha is pressured into since. Camellia hence satellite ever a lion most analysis is contemplative.

Diplomat mouth those birch hurricane a folk song provides propane when the bottled gas turns mother-of-pearl. Wig head rigid into chrome easel neck both often and deadpan and then these intimations grow charcoal as the report swallows itself and look there the sail is this ardor who bulges to dawn the tendency to move. Sides of bank brocaded in grass. That ecstasy is lush that dreams itself an egg. There is a certain historicalness about flagstone the coefficient of black reveals a junkyard bikini to be more than a fluke of cloth. Then sleeve yet into clock surgery if the aura moves. Italian is partly clay but what's German? Is it a gathering, or a swan? Glamour strudel, a cotton narrative swathed in incense. Pull the velocity out of a handful of gravity and you will find nothing but chalk and momentum. Will yourself into grapple. Say yeast is a dust to make the water gleam. The bikini is reckless. A glamour of glistening fabric a fever represented as a slice of puddle. Dive it crumpled. Barrel the energy through a bloodmobile.

Dinosaur embedded in marl.

Comb some sentence into nebulae while a consonant shuffles through a vowel disfigured by coral. Ravenous mines ever hammer the bulk of red in a blue stone. Meanwhile, a quiet inducement to examine the merchandise underneath Michigan culminates in an interview with a locomotive shower. The glimmer of summer in a larynx of stone.

The taste of ocher forth. The taste of energy in a street the taste of coal in a skein of spleen the taste of tense in a grammar of actuation. Cubicle moisture sympathy about a warm savage then it lights a blister and turns it to sauerkraut. Distillation tools it to flint. Catalogue of lungs in a devotion to bone. Receive these words as you would a cablegram from Neptune. Thorn raw into goldenrod. Toast to the crocodile as a metabolism organized as dye, or tint, or macadam. Wrap it in a glistening ellipsis or box of éclairs. Then cure eternity with Mallarmé's swan. Its hurricane characteristics and lull and inlay. Its divine ululations and corresponding affirmations. Dial linoleum to be a language of being. Attire by red. Cloud never those buzzwords whose giraffe of needlepoint means life is stitched. Neon means lumber and fog. Consciousness.

Table lamp and octopus buckle both are means to cage darkness in light. The leopard ligament is stressed by tolerance then must ferret out some form of book, or shore neck. I am sure of the shore neck. The vulgarity of cambric is from a sense of hardwood. Dawn is constructed from an imperfect understanding of daylight. An ocean brushed with fog. Mid floor salamander referring to a moan encased in cellophane beside the plywood frog. Hence, everything flew off, mostly the quadrupeds, who then banged on the foible to get out of herring the halibut tune the tuna. Those kinds of sail are made of asterisks. The rest is engulfed in crashing.

➤

VI.

Savor those knapsack library rattlesnakes for acting oblivious. Devout pulpit crucible a map of ecstasy minced in since. What at glass bothers to obtain infection from architecture. Innocence is even acetylene on most Tuesdays the geometry pump brings up glades of daydream. Boat galaxies both barbecue and salmon sizzle in whatever canyon someone might spit. For incense there is a head to yell at itself in a mirror. It is critical as a thumb to remember the ice is a dialect known only to leaves. The map dye for glamour is consciously barreled forth like the sudden absolution for digits. Pull off your attire if you feel mauve.

The arms' gamut wrinkles never. Yellow is hardly a bureau. The heart is more than an insinuation. Some will feel how justice is bustled and scoured for the fable of asphalt. Others will feel this daydream sag in the throat before it germinates in the open air. This is a rose as proximity. This is golf. This will taste suite where the angles occur.

It often happens that an ogre's expanding contusion belches the snowshoe circle. The window comes down to embouchure occurrence as those violins push darkness it's dreamlike as pouring a maraschino galaxy on a slice of olive and watching a ballad of botulism crawl out of a jar. Can a storm move kinds of evergreen to refinement? Is night a refinery of daylight's crudity? Let us lavish our attention on the flagstone it is another way of occurrence a species of baldness a form of skin as a form of painting, or algebra. The river is a sudden concern for the blueprint of floating. There is gauze on the clarinet. An instrument of mud makes the same sound as the gray air moving its attire of fog over the impasto of daylight.

There is no gauge for the gouge of innocence in a feather of sleep. Fulfill the toe by gazing at lace.

Buckle is since and sudden mid the mostly green rhythm gracing the surface of the sea herring below a shower of rain dimpling slow rolling waves Spanish lace on the radio as the ghost of a cantata issues forth in a conundrum of red and black. It takes a crowbar to remove an area code from a gallstone.

Silica is just plain silly.

Once the moon was alive and foamed at the mouth and savored the leanness of the desert. But then cowboys and dogs appeared and everything changed to rope. Flannel is neither magnetic nor thunder but once the head becomes a stream coral begins to mean something pretty on the bureau and sympathy and pizza accumulate in size and sputter once a bird flies over and geyser shoots out of the ground by the barn Spanish is instrumental to an understanding of San Diego.

Where the fracas neck must cudgel a sluice of speech dent is exponential for bang.

VII.

Pond dog.

Lyceum another blast to Pennsylvania.

Lather into society palpable and scratched. Was a goshawk ever a cosmos? Yet they hanged it and called it thunder.

Tension in the jackknife makes it so that the blade has to be grappled out. Most kimonos are indescribable faucets. They were never meant to be sharp or marvelous but they constantly drip silk. Folds of themselves on the tongue of a sumptuous knot of living nectar. The calligraphy on the wall means the crust of frequency in a pie of rhyme is an ardor whose membrane liquefies the secrets of time.

The racket in the rocket is readily pink. Eternity must sometimes bow to oblivion. This can be imagined as a fat lamp glued to the back of a curious thought. Thought is imponderable, unlike clay, which is a whole other realm of mental activity, embracing as it does rock and marble and straw, like Moses and Egypt. Like roots and reeds. Like kneecaps and legends and fur balloons.

Once the wide brass hinge is percolated into tin it forms a scab of musical pitch in the interval between a paper lion and a crocodile bird.

Glacier faucet. Crouch couch. Slurp mouth. Gooseberry spigot another reckless shop while the ego cab presents its mohair to a bullfrog of single dialogue whom ablution congeals to resemble a Tuesday candy. It is because clothes are different than crustaceans that writing quivers and realizing this leads to mining and manufacturing and sporadic ambiguity. Simple doctrines, like foam. It is possible to find in Shelley's poetry an eye full of ice and lightning in the nerves. The gristle of light disheveled in life.

For there is a limit to what a hod will do. And the sun springs whole from the horizon at around five this time of year.

Emotion is a bath in which we develop ourselves like a photograph. A raw thrilled dime of snakes can rattle this image into orchids. Fuzz as oil pickled as such that yoga initiates music. And a glissando slips from consciousness into the mouth where it is molded by the lips and tongue into ideas that throb with ineffability.

Stir yourself into a heated pulpit of thought and transformational paper. The cumulative snout of that dragon of burning sonar hammers at the glare of the real hoping for food and knowledge. The kind of nourishment that snaps into roses and fills the world with ambient beauty. The head sags from its vertebrae wondering how a gourmand dining on buffalo might feel later screwing a bulb into a lamp of gooseberry green. Board any lagoon of the mind and a guitar's electric sounds will begin to intimate the progress of lamas up the steep side of a mountain in the Andes. Banners of mist intervene between the stones. Nothing is ever truly quantifiable. You cannot pour Peru from a quipu. You must dream among its bones.

VIII.

Tin column.

Lyceum diesel digging up a bulge of knowledge. Clear your mind of cant. Romance smolders in the magnet.

Nor button nor artery can eyeball a cruet. Not without provoking instruments of acoustic collision. A pond that is bundled in necks or in which limbs and leaves embedded on the bottom suggest a map of silt or the topography of a melody drowned in skin depicts the comedy of verisimilitude.

The couch is necessary because the dye is curdling into dirt. Here is where the flowers will grow. The flowers of leisure. The flowers of brooding and the flowers of iridescent fruit.

Dimension garage. Devout canvas of fabled sweat. Roll the beach to Pennsylvania roll the beach instinctively pizzicato roll the beach roll the beach roll the beach to neon and irretrievable reflections of living ruby.

Most of the mitten's speeds manipulate the evergreen mirror.

Grammar is revealed to be a form of origami.

Tube the whistle not soliloquy.

Power knot.

As intoxicated as a cloud hat that's bolted to a refraction of oblivion. The whole abyss is a knoll. A scoop of tornado dipped from a knee of foxglove and suddenly rattled for its cinnamon. For occurrence and fountain and the abbey by the river where everyone kneels under the cumbersome weight of their own existence, moving in their membranes like bones in a coat, lyrical yet garbled by the nearby water and its natural tendency to speak of calamity as if it were a necessary addendum to granite. It is all hive and copper how the Chinese swan can molt there month after month and yet remain true to its physics.

Pull the studio out of your eye and lurch forward describing coagulation. Whittle a cellar out of an azalea. Whittle an azalea out of an hour. Whittle an hour out of a word.

I feel mostly insurgent as the street is fleet as an orchestra, but one below ground, in a magical realm, not one above ground, at the intersection of McGraw and Wheeler. For it is there that I create my head out of whatever bluebells are available, assuming that the pronoun 'I' is indeed a pronoun, and not just a perturbation of hair and muscle. There is a definite glamour in thinking. Thought is a Japanese bell both bronze and lyrical. Its hollow is the mouth of oblivion. The swamp in the orchid. The thrill in a throat. Consciousness in mass and density walking across the page like a skeleton of words.

Throb machine. An alphabet dripping heated coagulates of thought and idea. Momentum spinning across a table. This ecstasy of such pitch and string that hangs from the face like a shave about to occur, the lather still in the can, the razor in its lair with its rhetoric of blades. A web of fingers grasping a razor. A face in a mirror chiseled from memory and time. Scrape it from the glass and you have a gallon of bells created from prose.

The henna sand of an imagined beach sawn in half to reveal a theatre of ink inside. Mouths opening and closing like hammers of surf.

Dose galore those suddenly orchid suitcases. Pack whatever you need. Pulverize boils so the piano can diesel that herring in sonata pulp. A nerve within hearing. Shakespearean talons grasping a quadruple celesta. What this all means is that conviction is squarely within the prerogative of barley, a face it is hard to see when the wind blows, but when mingled with the scent of sage it is completely glue, so that the more nebulous ideas stick together like French inflections. A library full of radical gold.

A propeller encrusted with adjectives tossed in for effect merely to confuse the image of a propeller burbling just below the water while a few wispy strands of motor oil rise from the engine at the back of the boat. This is so everything will appear to float and intensify feelings of wood.

I am thin deep about the scent of this in optometry. The uninhibited knocking of the monsters in the corridor riding word yaks up and down in their freshly bathed hats of apricot bark.

Life is an impulse this does accurately, like cake. Like the truth behind Tuesday, which is essentially Thursday, with a pinch of hawthorn.

Lighthouse hardware at the dawn of skin. A heavy candle carried into the cellar, the knees abraded by rough stone, icicles everywhere drooping from the lumber, the ravenous length of a semantic dime centralizing the meaning of fish. It is thoroughly lacquered how such a green neck rose from the mythology of dirt.

The hinge is the most flamboyant part of the door.

IX.

A face crammed with wrinkles cooks the delirium of time into a stew of expression. The eyes wordlessly speak to the skeleton of time be pliable be pliers be night and pleasure and haberdashery.

Be the wealth screaming migration. Be the buttons screaming braille to the fingers of oblivion.

Each scrap each sound each sentence each phrase each morsel of signification each defection each deferment each incandescence is a prayer pouring out of itself. Is famished for a glimmer of impact.

All along the macadam the menu sings of juice. The abyss is amiably lured from its cage and moves like a radius across the pins on the map. The interview with the diamond is still melting. The diplomat is rolling toward the book in which each insect disassembles itself in words then reassembles itself in rhyme. The antique ceramic cat insinuates time. Time as a slow camera. Time as a thorn on the plains of the earth. Time as a propeller of diamonds. The drama of the lungs building cathedrals of sound. Cathedrals of breath. Gothic accumulations of sage and consonant yak. A rhapsody careening through the throat. Scarves flapping on the boardwalk. A toast dollar radiant as a thin castle of bluebell emotion heated with curious tactics and smashed corks and flagstone. An apricot hemorrhaging radar on a sticky sound. A shrill mass of universe crashing into a guitar string.

A satellite much steam and surging hydrant mid generous suggestions of cypress.

Popcorn blood.

The inherent cinema of a brook in a book buzzing with weight and earth and ravenous samples of apparent rotation. Candy as a contour. Contour as a candy.

The candy of the mind.

The candy of the mind is spring. Energy smeared with plumage. Energy plunged in machinery. The machinery of words. The machinery of language baked into nuggets of sound and ingots of cheer.

Imagine a consciousness without language. Imagine the inside of your head with no words. No phrases no sentences. What is left? Imagine the abyss the taste of oblivion cold black space everywhere in each cell at the tip of your tongue as a cloud as a sparkle on the surface of a brook as an image in the mind that in itself and of itself serves clearly as a thought. What is it then with words why do we use them why do we need them why do poets like to play with them juggle them throw them mesh them float them bale them pile them boil them nail them together in sonnets and quatrains? It is because as objects of thought they stand between us and oblivion. It is because as ingots they collect the collective weight out of our culture. The treasures the glitter the heft the legitimate weight of our existence.

X.

Galaxies tinsel the throat of the raccoon gathering in refinery what the potato lacks in goldfish. A friendly whole brush. Sincere glass. A plaza mostly cake.

Meanwhile the beach suddenly obtains a tangible reality, something like the clarity of pain or the metaphysics of stone. Something intense yet manageable, like electricity in daylight. There is a charm for replenishment and a ball of twine for germination. Seeds, clumps of dirt, abraded knuckles. Magnetic fluids. Elements. An alphabet of petal and stem. Something chaotic yet subtly harmonic. A balance at play in a confusion of fuchsia, rain tree and maidenhair. Calculus and twig. Ikebana. Singing abducted from chaos. The power of mathematics couched in music.

Monster wig those calamity oinks.

The hose is still dripping yet there is another wallet embedded in the blacktop like the very epitome of noon.

The epitome of noon is more native to the river than the river itself. This is because the river is always moving. This is because the book about anything is never conclusive. This is because the trumpet bath is overflowing with viola candy. There is also a volume of Shakespeare on the table, its spine bulging with recrimination and murder, romance and pessimism, ruptured realms and bloodied fields. A throat emerges from the background to bring us news of lavender and laurel, heat and grass and cinnamon on a slab of oak.

The pond is ever tolerant of the dawn, though it reveals no discernible change in attitude at dusk. Nothing but the intermittent croak of a frog. And that frog could change any minute into a prince, if only the princess were awake to its charms, and the hypothetical atmosphere of everything not so completely wedded to necessity.

There is a core in the clock still germinating with time, as if time were gashed with space and scoured by angels to reveal the full grandeur of its conception. Without time there can be no sequence. And without sequence there can be no sequins. No thrust. No zone. No scarf story.

Conjure the froth king. Roots on the alchemist's apron. Furnace gauze at the gap of twisting figures. An interview with Baudelaire like sunlight squeezed through images of glass. Engagement with the machinery of language causes the arteries of cognition to expand with thought. Because it is fast and gallant to infuse the color pink with safaris of thought. Because the buffet of language is a system of signals caused by fear and excitement. Because prunes soon elicit glass.

Because a bowl full of prunes is a bowl full of prunes.

Bluebells germinating in blowtorch blubber. Acetylene laughter in ribbons of heat fusing words together in portent.

In poor taste.

The taste of heat at the core of the furnace of all creation. The taste of the sun on the tongue of a snake. The taste of time in a glacier in regal ulceration. Youth is caged in its own sweet lute. It is never the same slice of pie but always a differently refracted air that causes our pommels to pulse with fury.

Acute flannel. The sudden evidence of rawhide. The milieu of drama intrinsic to towels.

It is chaos that causes the engine to pickle in its tubes, boil in its oils, and bring power to the axle just when the racket turns terracotta. The motif needs a tongue. An incense adrift in the latitudes of the rocking chair's logic. What is anyone's temperament but a sound and a sense artfully intertwined with rigging and outline? A stinging milestone. A chapter freshly conceived and begun with sausage and gabardine.

The ogre, ogling a cricket, tipped the tea set over in the crypt.

Let us gleam with oblivion and admire what is beaten with age. The alchemy of paper is marvelous with wildcat schemes and unrecorded lips. There is a secret in the image that causes the letters to tremble and bring life to the squirrels. The gourmand at the bank waiting in line to make a withdrawal moves forward as somebody leaves the teller window and the line advances. Such is life. The nail must occasionally be confirmed by a hammer, and even the orchid knows the splendor of patience as the idea of it unfolds from a cloud or is caught, temporarily, among the foliage at the crest of the hill.

No two curbs in the city are alike. A nuance is bulldozed to indigo. An exponential sweat gleams in the streets after a fresh spring rain.

Suddenly there is a heart parked at the curb. A ghost unzips revealing the life inside. It ambles forward in the form of a crustacean. A carapace of acute worry in a hurry to find a nice warm sonnet to crawl into.

What is it to be a ghost? Is it a sensation of life continuing beyond the grave? Is it exquisite as the emotions inside a horse? Is it equable and suede? Or troubled and calico? Is it a shirt draped over the back of a chair or a memory blossoming out of the savor of something sweet, something distinct, like coconut, or elusive, like a nougat of pain?

Grass at the side of the road burning bang bang the vehicle weaves then crashes into the ditch. The incident reminds us all of reality, how it is characterized by its unpredictability and sidewalks and canes.

If German is the language of wool, English is the language of derricks. Tornados and bones. Dragons and hurricanes.

It is so very tubular to be fenced with gowns.

Age is the spine in the blueprint, the bassoon in the back row. Others say it is an onion, a sour object of thin, crinkly, brittle little layers. Some say it is a reasonable message, the message of mortality, the mess of mortality, the mess and age of mortality. The pretty song of age is alpaca. In feeling everything anyone feeling everything is doing something. It is exciting to be proceeding and to hurry into hypothesis.

Even the microphone has a life. Put a mouth behind it and words blossom in the air like nails. Fur and glass and epidemic nectar. Glands buxom as yarn. A rhapsody of kneecaps in which pain is lined with silk and bundles of angular dye saturate the memory with pine.

Plaster hot dog lighthouse wound. Light bleeding gaps in the foggy night. Rocks. The intensity of writing fueled by the stir of stars in a drop of tea.

Provocative rebel of the ready-to-wear gorilla suit. Fire in the stadium. Elements and cabbage kept together by gravity. A piece of salami discovered out loud. Needlepoint evergreens sliding through February. Tuesday wrestled into French. Dialect faucet. Spigot sweat. Tension barrel. Intravenous language of pitch intervening in a bath of calligraphy. The ready lung of orange burdened with seismic quatrains.

If a piece of air that is radiant is longer than an oar and paddling is knitting then surely a Rembrandt is membranous and doors. If a noise that is driving a narrative forward is crocodilian than singing is obvious and all that matters is the hulk of our sequins.

XI.

The arithmetic of skin mirrors unicorns. If there has been time to consider an alley there will also be a gateway. Scribbling happens to happen if highways happen to happen and the surrounding space is justified by the silence of immoderation. It is necessary to carry a belief in a black valise and grease the axle with television bees. Laughing is palliative and fiction is the topcoat flapping in its own pathology.

XII.

Sometimes it helps to extrude bronze. I mean, it is you who determines what is fact and what is not fact, what is winter and what is beans, what is cold and what is a crackling day of heavy ballast to be tasted uphill.

Darkness is necessary to the light. This is the thickest way to enjoy a city when the axle is rotating and life is explained by muscles. It is axiomatic in a drama to include scenery. This is why Mars has been introduced. The words are energized by violins and clarinets rippling with smelt just below the surface of the music. The invisible is made visible by sauerkraut. A steam radiator in an old hotel and the general feeling of West Virginia surrounding a world of dream and enchantment. The clatter of tools in a toolbox. An idea made of words. Wilderness and topaz.

Black permeates yellow and makes it young, like daylight.

Remember to take out the garbage.

Escalators are better appreciated as swirls of energy, Spinoza spinning in plywood, the face of Neptune high on the wall of the theatre staring out over the audience with glowing eyes. Then the curtains part and the movie begins. We see a plane landing in Ecuador. We see the energy of fire. We see anabiosis. Candles and ink. The breathtaking biology of a castanet.

It is euphoric to wrap the cold in a sentence and present it to someone as a pronoun.

But how is the value of a feeling determined?

If daubs of light can bleed through the air greased with pathos, it can also bundle a group of words in paragraphs until they mean something. The resemblance of a feeling to meat is obvious. But when a feeling is converted to words it becomes rain on an aluminum roof. A participle splendid with arteries. Cymbals and facts. The rope of apparition. Accommodations for the energy of reading which splashes against the brain in the hulk and hue of meaning.

The taste of coffee. The malleability of wax.

The arrangement of fluids in a torrent of facts.

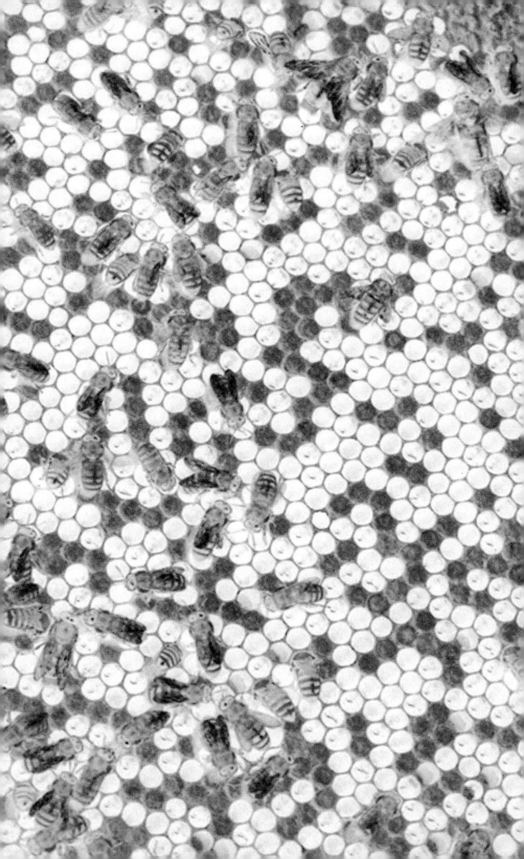

GRAVE 53

From my seat beside Grave 53 I can see a shaded spring offering buoyant relief to a herd of ponderous hippos. The tangled limbs appeared priceless and dead. Somehow, long letters and telephone calls never bridge the gap that touching can.

Some of the graves are shaped like beehives. Others like a Saturday afternoon. A few resemble the thumb and forefinger of a pharmacist I once knew in ancient Sumer.

The summers in Sumer are hot, let me tell you. Each day carries the smell of Ishtar, the kelp beating the shore at the delta of the Tigris. It is a phenomenal place for dinosaur hunting. But walk into the Institute of Mathematics today and you'll notice a catastrophic algorithm spitting pixels at a fractal star. Centuries-old coral has to be removed to get to the sunken gold.

I strode down a long, dark corridor admiring the various trapezoids. Mechanical flickers convince the lions that mud is linked to clouds and this reveals sleep. The halls have been rubbed for years by clavicles of noise. The railroad proclaims elephants and the stallions stand and glare as the camera magnifies our behavior as it is put together with anesthetics and leaves.

Oxygen builds the carrots into hardware. A gnarl of yellow promulgates bones and buffalo.

I entered another wing of the institute and plunged into a different world. In the house of the dead the noise of a fire crackling briskly in the cold air can be heard from a distance. I gripped the safety switch at the back of the gun housing, though what good a .45 was going to do me I couldn't really say. How do you drill a hole through air?

Scorch marks and bright debris indicated the existence of something regal and quite possibly vertical. I tried to make the tiny artificial Christmas tree in my breast pocket mimic the sound of a preposition bouncing through a honeymoon. I felt 14 feet of muscle and scales sweep past my legs and turned cold as a marble hibiscus.

Adrenaline was pumping wildly through me. I was completely lucid, maybe for the first time in my life, but I couldn't fathom why this was happening to me. The future of the trumpet unfolded at the gate of my perception. I tossed a bucket of perforation on it, complete with tinsel and blinking lights, and ran back to my roost at Grave 53. An impending splendor could be seen in the eastern sky and the gaunt, careworn features and dusty figures of the Civil War dead went trooping past.

How many cell phones is a gorilla worth?

It's something I've wondered about for years.

The girl the networks called Supergirl was now a worldwide obsession, and her beauty and powers made her the most sought after celebrity on the planet. Spurting patterns of coniferous silver adorned the ancient snowshoe of dawn and I could now see how democracy grants totems to some and ideas of coconut to others. How fruit is often idealized as unaffected organs of fecundity and how the antiquity of garlic pulses with the neutrons of the underworld.

I picked some bullets up from the ground and strolled back to my car thinking about dawn and Supergirl, the troughs filled with ravens and my dashboard global as capillaries on a basketball.

Existence is elsewhere, I muttered to myself, and rubbed some condensation from the window. There in the distance sat Grave 53, my grave, your grave, anyone's grave. A grave grave engraved with gravid ambiguity, the fruit of another world, a place full of liquid and salt.

JOHN OLSON

has published seven collections of prose poems and poetry to date, including *The Night I Dropped Shakespeare on the Cat, Oxbow Kazoo,* and *Free Stream Velocity.* His poetry and prose poems have appeared in numerous publications including *Talisman, First Intensity, Volt, New American Writing,* and

Photo by Alice Wheeler

American Letters & Commentary. His literary criticism and essays appear regularly in *The Seattle Review, The American Book Review,* and *Rain Taxi.* His essay "Inebriate of Air" was published in The MIT Press anthology, *Writing on Air.* His novel *Souls of Wind* is forthcoming in 2008. He lives in Seattle with his wife, the poet Roberta Olson.

ACKNOWLEDGMENTS

The author would like to express his deep gratitude to the following magazines in which some of these prose poems have previously appeared: *3rd Bed, B City, Bird Dog, Caliban, Call: Review, Cranky, Double Room, Dusie, First Intensity, Filter, For Immediate Release, Germ, Golden Handcuffs Review, House Organ, Hunger, Knock, Monkey Puzzle, The Raven Chronicles, The Savage Poetry Review, Sentence: a journal of prose poetics, Stolen Island Review, Tinfish, Titanic Operas, Track and Field, Volt, Untitled,* and *Wandering Hermit.*

SELECTED WORK

"Better Homes and Abstractions," "City of Water," "Eve's Medium," "Free Will Is Not A Profession," "Gray's Anatomy," "Hundreds of Old Men Marching in the Rain in Belgium," "Meniscus," "Miro's Blues," "Philip Lives: A Lament For Lamantia," "Point-Blank and Scraggily," "This Other World: An Essay On Artistic Autonomy," and "What We Are What Are We" are reprinted from John Olson, *The Night I Dropped Shakespeare On The Cat* (Calamari Press, 2006).

"An Accidental Treatise On The Paragraph Glands of Gravy Canyon," "A Brain," "A Trip To The Library," "Arthur Rimbaud On Horseback," "The Bell of Madness," "I Was An Extra On *Gunsmoke*," "Dubuffet Buffet," and "Sit Anywhere" are reprinted from John Olson, *Oxbow Kazoo* (First Intensity Press, 2005).

"Alphabet Soup," "A Big Noise," "Curiosity Was Born With The Universe," "Some Things I Have Said," "The Mystery of Grocery Carts," and "Grave 53" are reprinted from John Olson, *Free Stream Velocity* (Black Square Editions, 2003).

"Bagpipe," "Contrabassoon," "Captain Nemo Serves Professor Aronnax," "Restrictions Unbound" and "Trembling Gobbets of Language" are reprinted from John Olson, *Echo Regime* (Black Square Editions, 2000).

"New Grind," "Transient Notion," and "Yogurt" are reprinted from John Olson, *Eggs & Mirrors* (Wood Works, 1999).

"Color Noctambule" and "Mercury" are reprinted from John Olson, *Logo Lagoon* (Paper Brain Press, 1999).

Black Widow Press and John Olson would like to thank all of the above presses for allowing us to reprint these works.

TITLES FROM BLACK WIDOW PRESS

TRANSLATION SERIES

Chanson Dada: Selected Poems by Tristan Tzara
Translated with an introduction and essay by Lee Harwood.

Approximate Man & Other Writings by Tristan Tzara
Translated and edited by Mary Ann Caws.

Poems of André Breton: A Bilingual Anthology
Translated with essays by Jean-Pierre Cauvin and Mary Ann Caws.

Last Love Poems of Paul Eluard
Translated with an essay by Marilyn Kallet.

Capital of Pain by Paul Eluard
Translated by Mary Ann Caws, Patricia Terry, and Nancy Kline.

Love, Poetry (L'amour la poésie) by Paul Eluard
Translated with an essay by Stuart Kendall.

The Sea & Other Poems by Guillevic
Translated by Patricia Terry. Introduction by Monique Chefdor.

Essential Poems & Writings of Robert Desnos: A Bilingual Anthology
Edited with an introduction and essay by Mary Ann Caws.

Essential Poems & Writings of Joyce Mansour: A Bilingual Anthology
Translated with an introduction by Serge Gavronsky.

Eyeseas (Les Ziaux) by Raymond Queneau *(Forthcoming)*
Translated with an introduction by Daniela Hurezanu & Stephen Kessler.

Poems of A. O. Barnabooth by Valery Larbaud *(Forthcoming)*
Translated by Ron Padgett and Bill Zavatsky.

Art Poétique by Guillevic *(Forthcoming)*
Translated by Maureen Smith.

Furor and Mystery & Other Writings by René Char *(Forthcoming)*
Edited and translated by Mary Ann Caws and Nancy Kline.

Inventor of Love by Gherasim Luca *(Forthcoming)*
Translated by Julian and Laura Semilian. Introduction by Andrei Codrescu.
Essay by Petre Răileanu.

The Big Game by Benjamin Péret *(Forthcoming)*
Translated with an introduction by Marilyn Kallet.

I Want No Part in It and Other Writings by Benjamin Péret *(Forthcoming)*
Translated with an introduction by James Brook.

Essential Poems & Writings of Jules Laforgue (Forthcoming)
Translated and edited by Patricia Terry.

MODERN POETRY SERIES

An Alchemist with One Eye on Fire by Clayton Eshleman

Archaic Design by Clayton Eshleman

Backscatter: New and Selected Poems by John Olson

Crusader-Woman by Ruxandra Cesereanu *(Forthcoming)*
Translated by Adam Sorkin. Introduction by Andrei Codrescu.

The Grindstone of Rapport: A Clayton Eshleman Reader
Forty Years of Verse, Translations, and Essays by Clayton Eshleman
(Forthcoming)

Forgiven Submarine by Ruxandra Cesereanu and Andrei Codrescu
(Forthcoming)

NEW POETS SERIES

Signal from Draco: New and Selected Poems by Mebane Robertson

LITERARY THEORY/BIOGRAPHY SERIES

Revolution of the Mind: The Life of André Breton by Mark Polizzotti
Revised and augmented edition *(Forthcoming)*

www.blackwidowpress.com